1979

The Policeman's Art

FOUNDATIONS OF CRIMINAL JUSTICE

FOUNDATIONS OF CRIMINAL JUSTICE

THE POLICEMAN'S ART

AS TAUGHT IN THE

NEW YORK STATE SCHOOL FOR POLICE

by

GEORGE F. CHANDLER

with a new preface by

Marvin Boland

AMS PRESS
NEW YORK, 1974

Library of Congress Cataloging in Publication Data

Chandler, George Fletcher, 1872-
   The policeman's art.

   (Foundations of criminal justice)
   1. Police.   2. Criminal law.   I. Moore, Albert B.
II. New York (State). State School for Police, Troy.
III. Title.   IV. Series.
HV7921.C47   1974   363.2   70-156009
ISBN 0-404-09172-5

Foundations of Criminal Justice Series
General Editors: Richard H. Ward and Austin Fowler,
John Jay College of Criminal Justice

Published in the United States by AMS Press, Inc.
56 E. 13th Street, New York, N.Y. 10003

Manufactured in the United States of America

Quality in a Time of Crisis

A Preface to the New Edition of

THE POLICEMAN'S ART

If America were a society without poverty or com-
peting pressure groups, where everyone was happily in-
tegrated into the social structure, there would be little
need for police. Of course such an ideal society neither
exists nor is likely in the foreseeable future. It is obvious
that not only are poverty and special interest groups a
fact of American life, but there are a host of related social problems in education, housing, employment, and
equal opportunity in general that make America a complex economic-political-social battleground in which
there is not only the need for police, but for a mature,
competent, disciplined, sensitive, and responsive police.
The civil rights struggles of the 1950s, the riots and
social upheavals of the 1960s lend vivid support to this
need.

Our society has undergone considerable change since
the turn of the Twentieth Century. Population
movements have been from the farms to the cities, from
the East to the West, from the South to the North. We
are more industrialized and more highly specialized.
Our people have smaller families, more education and
live longer. Racial and ethnic, labor and professional,
political and civic interest groups are highly organized
and active. There is more frequent contact with the
police in non-criminal situations.

One result of these changes has been a breakdown
in respect for law enforcement because the nature of

our democratic society subjects the police to public scrutiny and investigation, leaving them open to criticism from all quarters. Release of information that is usually hidden from the public in closed societies—e.g., the recent Knapp Commission findings, grand jury investigations, Senate and Congressional hearings, watchdog committees and the like—leads to a widespread belief in the existence of police corruption and inefficiency. Indeed even the very concept of "law-and-order" is suspect today, since among some the concept is synonymous with repressive police action against minorities.

Another result has been a change in the role of the police and an identity conflict among the policemen themselves. With respect to role, the police are now more peacekeepers than law enforcers, with only a comparatively small percentage of their time devoted to the activities of criminals. The larger role is one of providing services designed to protect the peace and safety of the community ones, such as traffic control, handling accidents and ambulance cases, settling disputes and policing parades, strikes, demonstrations and crowds. As to identity conflict, there are questions of legitimacy of authority, loyalty to corrupt hierarchies in the police agency and the government, loyalty to courts and governmental heads who would jeopardize policemen's lives by making their jobs more difficult, sympathetic identification with struggling groups, and the "tough cop" versus the "social-worker cop" approach in role realization.

A good policeman today must have something more than his predecessor in terms of qualifications and preparation for this profession. Rigid selection standards will, no doubt, be even more demanding in years to come. It is increasingly essential, most experts agree, to recruit not only good physical specimens but candidates with higher education, greater intelligence, and more mature judgment.

Generally speaking, police training has not kept pace with social needs over the years, neither in amount nor quality. Training must be accorded higher priority. Heretofore thought of as solely job-oriented preparation, police training is increasingly being treated in a broader sense as professional preparation with both educational and vocational aspects. The recruit training programs of the largest American cities have reached the point where the educational component actually exceeds the vocational.

While this trend portends well for the future, police administrators have not yet resolved a more basic problem—that of input versus output quality. It has been clearly demonstrated in several well-known studies that a better quality output (police service) is probable, with less training, given a good quality input (police recruit), than a lower quality input with more training. Thus, police candidates recruited from colleges will, it is agreed, probably perform better as policemen with, say fourteen weeks of police training (as in the F.B.I. Academy for example), than candidates with less than a high school education after thirty-one weeks of training (as in the Chicago Police Department). An urgent need exists for analysis of this problem to determine the optimum educational/intelligence input level for maximization of output quality without the need for excessive and expensive training.

To understand the relationship of police performance to education, intelligence, training, and other factors, one must know something about both psychology and *The Policeman's Art*. Police work is truly an art, despite a significant increase in scientific aspects over the years, and it will always be an art, for the essence of the officer's task is dealing with an infinite variety of complex human problems. The quality of any program designed to prepare policemen for this task can only be measured in terms of how well those trained actually carry it out. It is important for police administrators to know what kind of training was given to a certain body of policemen with superior reputation. It is important to know historical developments in training: what has been or has not been tried, where, when, and under what conditions, results, and evaluations.

Such is one of the interesting things about *The Policeman's Art*. It tells of the development of police training in the New York State Police, the content of that training in 1922, and the experiences and reputation of that police agency. That the chapter on horsemanship is obsolete and those dealing with other matters are no longer applicable fifty years later because of new law, new equipment, or other developments, is beside the point. We learn from previous experience. We make progress in police work, as in other parts of our society, by change—by building on what is good and by laying aside what experience teaches us does not work.

Marvin Boland
Captain, 41st Precinct,
New York City Police Department

The Policeman's Art

As Taught in the New York State School For Police

BY

GEORGE F. CHANDLER

SUPERINTENDENT DEPARTMENT OF STATE POLICE
NEW YORK STATE

ASSISTED BY ALBERT B. MOORE
DIRECTOR NEW YORK STATE SCHOOL FOR POLICE

AND A

CORPS OF EXPERT COLLABORATORS

INTRODUCTION BY

AUGUSTUS S. DOWNING

ASSISTANT COMMISSIONER AND DIRECTOR
OF PROFESSIONAL EDUCATION
THE UNIVERSITY OF THE STATE OF NEW YORK

FUNK & WAGNALLS COMPANY
NEW YORK AND LONDON
1922

CONTENTS

Part II

By ALBERT B. MOORE

Lieutenant-Inspector New York State Troopers
and
Director New York State School for Police

INTRODUCTION

The importance of the mission which "The Policeman's Art" will perform in educating the people upon a subject with which most of them are not familiar has deeply impressed me. In our schools the education furnished to children and adults alike serves to take them out of the class of the illiterate and to put them into the class of intelligent citizens. However, it is only now and then that through an editorial or magazine article the subject of police is given any notice whatever. Even those charged with the enforcement of law and order are comparatively ignorant of police.

The authors of this book have realized all this during their conduct of the New York State School for Police. This school, organized by Major George F. Chandler, Superintendent of State Police, marked a new departure in the field of education, and it soon became evident that not only those who would become members of the police force, both in state and city, but the whole people needed to be instructed in the subject of the control and regulation of matters affecting the general comfort, health, morals, safety, and prosperity of the public.

"The Policeman's Art" furnishes this instruction, and the book should and must have a wide circulation throughout not only New York State, but throughout the entire country.

It gives me real satisfaction to commend this work as a text-book for study by both teachers and students alike and as a book worthy of careful reading by men and women interested in the welfare of the public. In the years to come the influence of this book for good will be far-reaching.

AUGUSTUS S. DOWNING,

Assistant Commissioner

and Director of Professional Education.

Albany, N. Y., July 1st, 1922.

PREFACE

POLICE is one of the most important developments of civilization. The detection and prevention of crime is not an exact science. It is an art. This book is simply a compilation of the more important subjects taught at the NEW YORK STATE SCHOOL FOR POLICE.

Underlying the teaching, we try to bring out the fact that a policeman is only a citizen who has chosen to be the servant of the public, one having no more and no less rights than any other citizen.

We maintain that the more intelligent he is, and the more he knows of police work, the less will he be an autocrat. He will realize his limitations, will know that a democracy is only as strong as its majority, and that in our country government is with and by the consent of the governed.

He will realize that he must work along prescribed lines, that he can not be used by any persons or organizations to coerce a citizen, or to settle personal grievances, or enforce private ideas of morality, but should give the maximum of protection with the minimum interference with the lawful rights of a citizen.

Penology, or the art of punishment, we feel should not be taught in a police school, neither should a policeman be interested in what happens to a prisoner after he is brought to justice. This is not his affair. Whether an "eye for an eye and a tooth for a tooth" is right or wrong is not for a police officer to decide.

Thanks are extended herewith to those officers and citizens who have so willingly given their time without remuneration as instructors in the school.

Their reward must lie in the knowledge that they are aiding to elevate the police to the dignity of a profession, and by so doing will increase the number of trained men who understand that liberty is the keynote of our country.

GEORGE FLETCHER CHANDLER,

Superintendent Department of State Police,

New York

POLICE is the name given to the administrative powers of a unit of civilization, or to the agents used to enforce such powers.

PART I

I

HISTORY AND OUTLINE OF POLICE

Law is supreme, and therefore the enforcement of the law or the maintenance of law is of the greatest importance in civilization. In fact, the enforcement of law or the police power of a nation is as necessary to its maintenance as food is to maintain the individual.

To maintain law or rules, monarchs or kings had only the men who fought to act as agents. The soldier, therefore, was the original policeman. As time went on, after the formation of the great Roman Empire, the emperors set aside a certain body of men to act as guards for their own personal protection. These, later, took on civil functions and acted somewhat like policemen. They were called the Pretorian Guards of Rome. A study of the use of these guards in Gibbons' "Decline and Fall of the Roman Empire" is well worth while. They were sometimes used for good and sometimes for political reasons. They were almost the first body of soldiers set aside to exercise certain police functions.

Gradually through the middle ages we have the development of the knights, and these knights going about the countryside on horseback, formed into groups, were actually the policemen of the middle ages. As they

13

disappeared, there came in their place the constable, or
man on horseback, going throughout the country, protecting against robbers and bandits. The word "constable" comes from the Latin words "comes stabuli,"
meaning "master of the horse." The original constable,
therefore, or rural policeman, was a horseman, and the
horse to this day is the policeman's greatest power as
a single instrument in the preservation of law and order.

Police as we know it to-day is of very recent establish-
ment, for it was not until 1829 that Sir Robert Peel, of
England, after years of work, succeeded in getting an
act through Parliament whereby all agents used to enforce the law were put under one head and uniformed
alike. This in cities. A year or two later a rural
police, the Royal Irish Constabulary, was formed. This
was the beginning of rural police in the world. Other
police systems were started in other countries and rural
police was formed in Australia, India, and in Canada,
until now practically all nations use them.

Uniformed police in our own country was organized
in New York City about 1850. There are men, therefore, alive to-day who were born before the advent of
police in North America.

The first rural police in North America was the Royal
North West Mounted Police, a very famous organization, organized by Major French, of Kingston, Canada,
in the year 1872. It is in existence to-day, tho somewhat changed. The next rural police in this hemisphere
were the Texas Rangers, 48 in number, a very wonderful organization backed up by the governor, for the preservation of law and order along the border of Texas.

The first real state police in the United States was the Pennsylvania State Constabulary, organized by Major John C. Groome in 1905, still in existence, having done splendid work from the beginning. The next to be formed was the New York State Police, in May, 1917. Now Michigan, West Virginia, Colorado, Massachusetts, New Jersey, all have state police or are organizing it, and the movement is growing throughout the United States.

Life is a strife—a battle—and certain basic principles of combat, which have been developed through centuries of military study, must be applied to it just as to every kind of warfare.

These principles apply to individuals who are fighting for personal success, and apply equally well to organizations which are fighting for successful development. So, too, they should be adhered to in the administration of a successful police force.

These military principles are nine in number:

(1) There must be one supreme commander.
(2) There should be one simple direct plan.
(3) The force must not be dispersed.
(4) If a detachment is sent for a particular purpose, enough should be sent to accomplish the mission and return intact to the main body.
(5) A reserve must be kept.
(6) Reserves must be used properly and at the proper time.
(7) Fire superiority must be maintained.
(8) Flanks must be protected at all times.
(9) Constant reconnaissance must be maintained.

These principles have come down through centuries, and are the basis of every successful command and of every successful organization, either civil or military.

Application of Principles

How well do these apply to the organization of a police force? Let us review them with their application to this subject:

(1) There should be one head. He should be absolute, and have all power over the men, the promotions, the organization and its personnel.

(2) He should have one simple direct plan and his orders should be simple. It is said that General Sedgwick, in the Civil War, had a fool on his staff to whom he submitted every order before issuing it. If the fool could understand it he would let the order go out.

(3) Forces should not be dispersed. Too many heads or precincts and too much division of authority make for weakness.

(4) Detachments of police when sent out for special work should be large enough to accomplish the result without needless danger to their own lives.

(5) Enough men should be kept on reserve for emergency.

(6) These reserves should be used only as a last resort to clinch a victory.

(7) Fire superiority, which in the army means getting advantage over the enemy's fire by proper shooting and volume of fire, applies as well here. In

a police force fire superiority would mean the prestige and authority of the police which make the crooks afraid of them.

(8) Flanks should be protected. By this I mean that the police department should be so carefully administered that there can be no real criticism of the force or its methods.

(9) Reconnaissance in a police organization means a constant keeping of accurate information at all times concerning activities of the crooks in the territory under its jurisdiction.

I believe that no police force to-day can be a potent factor in maintaining law and order as it should, unless it follows out these nine principles.

Raise the Police Standard

I believe that promotion should come from the ranks; that men who have made a success of their work should be rewarded. The service should be elevated. It should have a more practical uniform. The present clumsy uniform interferes with the activities of the average policeman. A policeman's revolver should be exposed where he can grasp it instantly when needed, and also for the psychological effect.

Every effort should be made to dignify and elevate the police service.

The Policy of the New York State Police

While studying the police problem it occurred to me that the work of a policeman and the work of a doctor are so similar that the principles are almost identical.

When a health law is broken by overeating or overwork, when a bone is fractured, or the breaking down of nature's defensive mechanism allows micro-organisms of disease to enter the system, then a physician is necessary. Likewise, should a law of civilization laid down by the State in which a person lives be broken by that person through stealing, killing another, or even minor infractions of the law, a policeman is needed.

Accidents or sickness may occur at any time during the day or night. So may lawbreaking. Therefore, a physician has no regular hours; he may be called at any time and should be ready to go at the call. It is the same with a policeman.

A physician has to build up a reputation by good work accomplished, and the policeman, too.

Both the doctor and the policeman must meet and understand all sorts of people; old and young, rich and poor, intellectual and ignorant, sane and insane. They must both avail themselves when in a hurry of any means of transportation to reach the scene of the trouble.

A physician must be a gentleman, kind, discreet, close-mouthed, active, and above all, he must know his business. These same qualities make the ideal policeman.

The work which a physician handles is divided into two great heads: the mechanical, which means surgery, and the medical, which has to do with the administering of drugs and with nursing. In addition, there are some special lines, such as nose and throat work, eye and ear pathology. The policeman's work has these same sub-divisions. The work of the state police in the rural districts I look upon as surgical. They should be sur-geons in a police sense, while the sheriffs, local con-stables, etc., are the general practitioners. Detective work, finger-print work, etc., come under the head of specialties.

The ordinary common ailments may be attended by the family doctor, but when a big accident occurs, or a bone is fractured, or a tumor or other foreign growth is suspected, it calls for a surgeon. So the work of con-stabulary is the big mechanical part of the work. They are called to police the great crowds which gather at the state and county fairs, to guard them against thieves and to prevent accidents. They handle the big traffic problems, and see to it that the licenses required by law are taken out so that the revenue may not be lost to the state. Murder cases, rioting and quarantin-ing in infectious diseases are their special line of work.

It has often been suggested that more plain-clothes work and detective work be done by police, but after careful observation, I feel that a different course is desirable. There must first be built up a prestige, in other words, a reputation for character, for the right type of man, for proficiency, certainty and surety of judgment in our work. This once attained, the work will come easier. As a physician gains a reputation, people come to him with confidence, and this is of ex-treme value to him just as it will be to a policeman. The mere presence of police is of great value through its

prevention of crime, entirely outside of the actual apprehension of criminals.

There is a saying, "Truth is sometimes stranger than
fiction," but on the other hand, fiction is much more
complicated than truth. In a detective story it is always
the most unlikely person who commits the crime. The
author covers up his trail with far greater care than
a real criminal does, and the reader must guess the
outcome by ignoring most of the evidence. In real
detective work it is usually the most likely person who
is the guilty one, altho finding him may be difficult
enough.

For example, the principals in a hold-up near Syra-
cuse were found and arrested by tracing carefully the
whereabout of a Ford car painted bright yellow. Who
would have thought that criminals would use such a
striking and unusual car as a means of transportation
when committing a crime? Yet such was the fact. No
fiction writer would have dared to use it. Our men,
instead of dismissing such an unlikely clue as impossible,
true to their teaching, followed it up and apprehended
the criminals. In studying the cases in reports, I
find that 90 per cent of our most brilliant work has
been accomplished by carefully following up the
obvious.

There are times when it is necessary in following clues
that plain-clothes men should be used. But should we
allow ourselves to be carried away by the fascination of
sleuth work, and let our police departments develop
into nothing but a detective agency, we would lose sight
of our mission, which, to my mind, is the doing of the

greatest good to the greatest number, with the least expense to the commonwealth.

There are those who may ask why the policy of police is not the same as that of the army. A police organization, while it is more ⌐ less military in its training, differs from the arm., ⌐ many very important aspects.

Each man on a police force is an army in himself. On duty he does not depend entirely on the orders of his superior officer. He must have initiative, he must make his own decisions, he must fight on his own responsibility. The art of strategy must be his, and he must feel sure of himself when he decides what to do. Except under certain conditions, every man is his own officer.

In the army, should a man go wrong, or be a disturber, or disobey orders, he is subject to court and guard-house. He can be forced to carry out orders. In police should a man be lazy or disobedient, or show unfitness in any way, he should be at once dismissed, for no man belongs on a police force who is not heart and soul in his work. This may seem a harsh procedure, but I believe it is the only course that will build up a successful force, and altho it precludes civil service, that to my mind is its greatest advantage, for civil service is the greatest obstacle to the advancement of police to-day.

A force that maintains law and order in any commonwealth should be a popular one, and should give the maximum of protection with the minimum of interference with the lawful rights of citizens.

Popularity means success. If the law-abiding citizens all have a good word for a police department and its individual members, half the battle is won, because the moral force exerted through good-will is invaluable. Big business recognizes this fact and so do professional men. The good-will of the people is absolutely necessary to the success of a police force.

One slip by an officer will do more harm than one hundred good deeds can efface. Human nature unfortunately is not constructive, but likes to tear down, so one mistake or one unworthy act on the part of a policeman will subject the whole body to criticism. The hero of to-day is the scapegoat of to-morrow.

A police officer should err on the side of leniency. It is unnecessary to threaten or speak harshly. We will have no man who is not at all times a gentleman and who can control himself.

Self-control means control over the other fellow. A peace officer has advantage over the ordinary citizen, so must not overstep the mark in the use of his authority.

The public wants every criminal brought to justice and cares nothing about a record for arrests. It is convictions that are wanted, for a conviction means that the arrest was warranted.

Patrolling, settling difficulties, investigation, looking out for insanitary conditions and cases of cruelty to animals and children are just as important as the detection of crime.

In a police officer, common sense is more than a virtue; it is invaluable. Putting yourself in the other fellow's place and dealing with him as you would wish a member of your own family dealt with, is a principle of good police work.

Professor William G. Sumner, of Yale, divided the people of the United States into four classes: A—The Rich Man, who has his money through inheritance, or has made it, whether honestly or dishonestly. B—The Poor Man, who, as a class, has little power. C—The Reformer, who by stirring up existing conditions makes his own living. Lastly (the largest class of all), D— "The Forgotten Man." He is the every-day citizen, the voter, the taxpayer, who gets nothing from A, helps take care of B, and practically supports C; in fact, he carries the load of the nation on his shoulders.

D, "The Forgotten Man," is the man whose servant the police should practically be. Let us put ourselves in his place. Let us treat him as we would wish to be treated ourselves, with courtesy, with fairness, and above all, with honesty. If he calls on us for service, give him immediate attention, no matter how trivial the request. It means much to him, little to us, but perhaps a great deal to our profession.

I do not mean that we can not be of use to A, B, and C. These classes are more prominent and naturally present themselves more frequently for our attention for service.

But it is D, "The Forgotten Man," the average American, who represents the people as a whole. If we treat him fairly and make him like us, he and his kind will line up solidly behind us to preach the motto of the New York State Police: "Obedience to Law is Liberty."

II

ORGANIZATION

In the study of police a general knowledge of organization is essential. The following rules or regulations for the administration of a force are given as a general working basis. They have been drawn up after a study of the best police organizations of this country and are necessarily very general in character. Adjustments must be made to conform to the size of the organization, and it must be considered whether the members of the organization furnish their own equipment and uniforms, or whether these are provided for them.

General Rules for a Police Force

1. The members of a police force will bear in mind that they are a preventive as well as a repressive force, and that the prevention of crime is of greater importance than the punishment of criminals. The force individually and collectively will cultivate and maintain the good opinion of the people by prompt obedience to all lawful commands, by a steady and impartial line of conduct in the discharge of its duties, by cleanly,

sober, and orderly habits, and by respectful bearing to all classes.

2. Each member of a department ought seriously to consider the totally new position in which he is placed through an appointment whereby he becomes a peace officer with its authority and powers.

3. Any military drill regulations may be selected to govern the mechanism of the organization. The law as laid down by the statutes, together with any manuals selected, should be used for guidance in the performance of its duties and should be conscientiously adhered to.

4. *Sanitation.* The person, clothing, equipment and quarters of the members of a department at all times will be kept in a sanitary condition. If horses are used, strict attention to the care of mounts, cleanliness of stables, and horsemanship in its broadest sense will be exacted.

5. *Equipment.* The improper use of property furnished to the organization will be summarily dealt with. Every officer is accountable to the chief for such property and in case of its being lost, spoiled, or damaged, otherwise than by unavoidable accident or an accident in service, will receive such punishment as may be agreed upon. Any officer who wilfully or through neglect suffers to be lost, spoiled, or damaged any property, must make good the loss or damage or be dismissed from the service.

6. *Liquor and Drugs.* No alcoholic drinks nor narcotic drugs shall be used by any member of this depart-

ment while on duty unless by proper authority, nor shall
such articles be kept upon the person or in the quarters of any policeman. No member of this force while
in uniform shall enter a public drinking place or dis-
reputable place except in the performance of his duty.

7. *Uniform.* The uniform shall be worn as prescribed at all times except on leaves of absence and
furloughs, or upon proper authority.

8. *Gratuities.* No gratuity or award shall be
accepted individually or collectively by the members
of this department, except by written permission of
the chief, who may direct its acceptance.

9. *Gambling.* Gambling in any form is strictly forbidden, and borrowing or lending money or equipment
among members of the force will not be tolerated.

10. *Canteens.* Canteens will be allowed subject to
the approval of the chief who shall direct the use of
funds derived therefrom and no alcoholic beverages will
be sold.

11. *Transportation.* Transportation will be furnished members of this command in the proper performance of their duty while on detached service with
the proper understanding before such duty.

12. *Roster.* Detached service shall be by roster.

13. *Correspondence.* All correspondence shall be by
mail. Telephone and telegraph or radio used only
where time is a factor for consideration and only on
official business. All correspondence shall conform to
some model agreed upon.

14. *Property Returns.* Property returns shall be

rendered on the first day of July and the first day of January, each year, or oftener at the discretion of the chief.

15. *Records.* All records, transactions and accounting shall• be prepared and forwarded to the office of the chief, and all blotters shall be kept up to the minute as directed.

16. *Reports.* Reports of all investigations of crime, apprehension of criminals, special duties or detached service, in connection with the work of this force, shall conform to a standard agreed upon.

17. *Publicity.* No information of any character pertaining to the organization or its work will be given out for publication either directly or indirectly except by authority of the chief.

III

PSYCHOLOGY AND LEADERSHIP

Psychology is the study of the cause of behavior. **If** a man stands near an ant-hill and drops a stone, he knows that the ants will all run away. Should he place a lump of sugar near the ant-hill, he knows that the ants will swarm around it. So, if a man standing in the window of a tall building should suddenly yell "Fire! Fire!" he knows that the people on the sidewalk below him will look up and start running in his direction. This knowledge is psychology.

Certain acts of yours or certain words spoken by you will produce certain reactions from others. If one studies such acts and results, he is a student of psychology.

Psychology comes from the Greek words "psyche," meaning spirit or mind, and "logos," speech. Therefore, psychology is a discussion about the mind.

Man has five senses: seeing, hearing, feeling, tasting, smelling, and only through these five senses can man communicate with his surroundings or be cognizant of what is going on about him. All normal people are endowed with these senses, but some are capable of using them to better advantage than others. We can not actually read a man's mind, but we may arrive at fairly accurate conclusions concerning its action. When you talk with any one you may think you know what is going on in his mind, but you do not know anything definite. It is only his actions, his talk, and what you see that make you believe what he tells you.

A blind man can not be a psychologist.

Memory, outside of the physical, is all there is to a human being. We eliminate spiritual discussion. Wipe away his memory and his identity is gone. A baby as he grows up gradually learns to use his senses, and by use of his senses accumulates memory, and this memory makes up his character. For example, take the word "bell." A baby sees the bell and remembers its shape. He feels it and knows how it feels. He hears it ring. After a while he hears the word "bell" which he associates with the shape and sound of the object. Then he learns later how to spell the word "bell," how to write it, and how to read it. These impressions form a word concept in his brain. And so it is with other objects.

As the child gets older the memory of actions is registered on his brain. Also, the results which follow actions, the qualities of people and of things, causes and effects, all make memory and lead to knowledge.

Should he get up in the morning and see a gray sky with a good deal of wind it unconsciously brings to him the memory that rain usually accompanies such a vision. He thinks that there will be rain, and may say so. His thoughts, therefore, are based upon the memory that he has gained through his five senses.

This is but a brief sketch of how memory is built up, and how the mind acts. There is one thing in this connection that we must never forget, and that is that underlying memory and behind each one's personality is the God-given attribute called "will." Every normal individual has the power to decide for himself what he will do, and the study of psychology must include in it this most important of all our powers.

The past is gone, all that is left of it is memory or records. The future is not yet here, and can not be reckoned upon with any degree of certainty. But the present is now. It is here.

Since the present only is ours, the great secret of success, according to Marcus Aurelius, is to perform each act or duty as carefully and well as though it were to be the last act of life.

The man who commits a crime, who does a wrong to his neighbor, who is crooked in a deal, can not be happy.

To be decent, honest and straightforward makes one live a pleasant life and enables one to enjoy work, play, and amusements, and (if blessed with good health) all the things that make life worth while.

We can be honest, decent, helpful policemen, or we can use our personal powers for evil; which it shall be depends on the wish and will of each individual man on the force.

The study of psychology is necessary in our profession. The knowledge that every man can decide for himself and must do so, is essential to a policeman, and the effect his actions, manners and personality have on those about him in the performance of his duty, must be understood by him.

Education along these lines is very helpful and has become an absolute necessity in maintaining law and order in organized society.

The old-fashioned patrolman with a club, sent out without preparation, is becoming a relic of the past along with tyrants who ruled by blood, teachers who wielded the rod, and police chiefs who but too recently used the so-called "third degree" on suspected and often innocent persons.

The keen, intelligent, educated policeman who understands human nature, knows the law, and can use his wits, is now coming into his own.

For a policeman, or any one else, I believe the only value of psychology is to know how to use it. Psychology is a much misused word, and many people speak of psychology and psychoanalysis who have not the faintest idea of what it is all about. It has become a fad of the day and cults have arisen which may or may not be of use. However, there can be no question about the value of knowing how to influence others. Personality plays a great part in this. What is personality? Personality of the right kind among other things implies good manners. By good manners we mean that a man should be himself, be natural, but conform to the customs of the society in which he lives. The man of strong personality has the faculty of making other people feel that he thinks they are of great importance.

If a man has good manners and can carry the idea to other people that he is interested in them, and in what they are doing, he has that wonderful thing called "personality." To some it is given in great measure and is natural, but it may also be acquired.

If a policeman wears an ill-fitting uniform and is dirty, he does not have a good effect upon those who see him, and this counts against the force of which he is a member. If a policeman is slothful and uncouth in his manner, this also acts against the organization. But, on the other hand, should one see an upstanding, alert, clean-looking policeman who is courteous and kindly in manner, one would form a high opinion of him and of his associates.

Suppose such a man should enter a hotel and by his appearance make a very favorable impression up to the time he sits down to eat. The illusion would be dispelled if he makes a noise over the soup, or eats with his knife, or covers his knife and fork with his great big hands, or takes a piece of bread and wipes it all around the plate and mops up everything. What kind of impression will he make upon those around him? They say that if you watch a man eat you will know what kind of man he is. I don't mean that there are not splendid men who are without manners, but in a police force it is particularly essential that a man should convey to those around him an impression which is for elevation of the force.

Insanity is defined as a prolonged mental state in which there is a change from the normal in feeling, thought, and action as a result of bodily disease. A hallucination is a mental state in which there is a creation in a man's mind of something that is not so. Martin Luther, when he threw the ink-bottle at the devil, whom he thought he saw, is a splendid example. An illusion is the manufacture in one's mind of something that is not what he sees, based on something which is actually there. As an example, a man going near a graveyard at night might think a white post or tombstone was a ghost. A delusion occurs when a man distorts a fact and it seems real to him. If a man asserted that an automobile which was actually going to the west was going to the east, and he believed it, it would be a delusion.

The definition of insanity and of illusion, delusion and hallucination are given here as a part of a general knowledge of the human mind that a policeman should have.

To be a teacher and to understand leadership, one must be a student of behavior and all that it means.

The psychological test made in the army to grade officers and men, showed that the highest type of brain, rated A, which as a rule meant the quickest, made the best administrator. Strange as it may seem, speed and accuracy seemed to go together. This was just the opposite of our former ideas on the subject. It is not the slow, so-called careful man who makes the least mistakes after all, it seems.

Major Bertram F. Duckwall, Medical Corps of the U. S. Army, has classified administrative officers or leaders into six types of men. A brief summary of his classes is as follows: First, the man who has a bad temper and flies off the handle easily. He gets purple in the face and works himself into a rage over trifles that are often the result of his own faulty instructions to those under him. He is a bully by nature, now a bully with authority. He keeps everybody in a state of fear, and it is a known fact that no one can do good work who lives in such an atmosphere. Such a leader is always having a fight on his hands and imagines that his subordinates are trying to play him false. He does not gage the psychology of those with whom he comes in contact, and as a leader he does not last long. He is the kind of officer who, should he lead his command into battle, would probably be shot in the back, by accident (?).

A second type of leader believes that he is all there is to a command. He prescribes every act and tells just exactly how he wants it done. He does not trust any one. He stifles all initiative. He will never receive suggestions, so the organization which he commands is never benefited by any one's else ideas. Such an officer is usually a hard worker, but he spends hours working out details of the way he wants things done instead of giving his time and his brains to the big problems of his command. Such a type is sometimes the product of too rapid promotion. His administration is usually a failure, for bitter criticism takes the place of instruction and snap judgments work injustice to those under him.

The third type is somewhat like the second, but besides planning out all the details of the work, he tries to do it all himself. He is the busiest man alive. Everybody likes him, for he works every minute doing other people's work and letting others loaf. Altho he is extremely conscientious, he really accomplishes very little, for he works in circles and there is no cooperation. His organization fails because it is impossible for one person to do all the work. His energy could be utilized under a good executive but as a leader he is impossible.

The fourth type is the commander whose main idea is to be popular with his men. He will grant every request he can without sufficient inquiry and sometimes resorts to some underhand method to defeat the matter afterward. He hesitates to hurt some one's feelings and dodges the main issue. He praises every one whether he deserves it or not, but when put to the test will not back up his own men for fear of hurting himself with the public or some one higher up. He is evasive and shifts his responsibility as often as he can. He is what the army calls "a bootlicker" and will disgust efficient men under him. His striving for popularity defeats its own ends.

The lazy administrator is the fifth type. He may have a very successful organization if his subordinates are the right sort of men. Thrown on their own responsibility, they develop initiative and keep things going sometimes very harmoniously. The trouble comes when something arises which demands decisive and energetic leadership. Then unfamiliarity with his own organization will cause his collapse.

In contrast with these types is the real leader. Major Duckwall thus describes him: "He takes charge, and with a few well-directed efforts soon has everything coordinated and working. Harmony begins to manifest itself from the time he assumes the helm. Such an administrator usually has a pleasing personality, seldom becomes angry, is just in his dealings with his subordinates and is enthusiastic in the work. His success is very largely due to the justice which he accords to those under him. Men work well in an atmosphere of impartiality regardless of the amount of work they have to do. He works for the organization, for its success and not for his own, being wise enough to know that a man stands or falls by the work of those under his direction, and the results achieved." Such a leader is loyal to his men and will fight for them rather than allow an injustice.

Be a psychologist and study your own behavior as well as the behavior of others, understanding that every act and word of yours will produce certain effects upon those who surround you.

Classify yourself and see what type of leader you are, and school yourself to be the right sort; for every policeman already, in his daily work, a leader of men.

IV

FIRST AID

In teaching First Aid the writer believes that too much detail is usually presented to the student. His experience as a surgeon in emergency work has given him the opportunity of witnessing mussy, theoretical procedures as a result of superficial knowledge.

Therefore, the general principles of First Aid are here set forth, and if these are remembered, common sense will dictate the rest.

Plainly speaking, the body is made up of a bony framework called a skeleton, which is held together by ligaments. Where the bones come together, joints are formed, and muscles are attached to the bones for movement.

Arteries and veins carry blood, nerves carry impulses; and in the great cavities of the head, thorax, and abdomen are the internal organs, such as the brain, lungs, stomach, and intestines.

The body is covered by skin and lined with mucous membrane, and this skin and membrane is Nature's great defensive mechanism.

What can happen to this body? Roughly speaking, only three things:

First, accidents. This word covers everything from

the minutest pin-prick to the greatest casualty, and includes burns.

Second, infection.

Third, new growths.

So long as nature's defensive mechanism is intact, there is no danger of infection. By this is meant that if the skin and mucous membrane is not broken, infection can not enter. An accident of any kind breaks this defense, and outside of the mechanical injury in itself, there is the danger of infection.

Every object in this world is covered with micro-organisms commonly called germs; little living atoms that can not be seen by the naked eye. They are on our hands, in our mouths, in our ears, on our clothes, and on every object that we touch. These little micro-organisms produce disease and blood-poisoning.

TO AVOID INFECTION, THAT IS, TO PRE-VENT THE ENTRANCE OF THESE DISEASE OR POISON GERMS INTO THE BODY, IS THE GREAT OBJECT OF FIRST AID.

We have certain known agents which will kill these micro-organisms, heat or fire being the best. There are also iodin, carbolic acid, bichlorid of mercury, and alcohol.

When called to the scene of an accident, the first thing you should do is to keep cool, speak calmly, and so quiet those about you. Assume the authority, remembering that you are not a doctor, but are there to do the necessary practical work until the doctor arrives.

Make a careful survey of the situation, for it is very easy to do the right thing.

Should there be bleeding, tie off with a handkerchief, or cloth, or rope, or strap, above the wound, but only tight enough to stop the hemorrhage. If this does not do it, try tieing it below the wound, for the bleeding may be from a vein. While doing this, find out where the nearest available doctor is, and have some one go for him. Do not send for several doctors at once, except in case of a great casualty.

If a hospital is within reasonable distance, it is best to take the patient there instead of sending for a doctor. This applies to accident cases only. If a person has become suddenly ill, or is found in an unconscious condition, simply put him in a comfortable position in a sheltered place, such as a house or ·barn, and wait until the doctor comes.

Make an injured patient as comfortable as possible and PUT NOTHING INTO THE WOUND unless aseptic. Should you have a first-aid packet with dressings that have been rendered free from germs (sterile as we call it), place these dressings against the wound in such a way that your hand does not touch the surface of the wound nor the surface of the dressing that is to be placed next to the wound.

Should you have iodin, pour some of it into the wound first. It is an excellent procedure, tho somewhat painful to the patient.

Should a bone appear to be broken, place a coat, pillow, or piece of board under the injured member, and fasten the member to the apparatus if possible. This is merely to make the patient comfortable. DO NOT TRY TO SET THE BONE.

Should there be bleeding from cuts about the head, the pressure of a sterilized dressing against the wound will easily stop it, and then a bandage may be applied by wrapping strips of cloth or anything else about the dressing to keep it in place. If one has no sterile dressing or first-aid packet at hand, take a piece of cloth and scorch it by fire (a match will do), and place this scorched cloth against the wound; it will do very well. Laying a piece of cloth on a stove, if it is handy, till the cloth is burnt brown, renders it sterile. This is an old-fashioned method, but a good one.

Avoid giving the patient food; but if there is no reason to suppose that an internal injury has occurred, a hot drink of coffee or tea should be administered, or possibly a few drops of spirits of ammonia in water if they can be obtained.

Loading up the patient with alcoholic stimulants is not good, for it masks the symptoms.

In the case of burns, take about a quart of boiled water into which put a tablespoonful of baking soda. Clean cloths may be dipped in this soda solution and placed upon the burn. The use of oil has been advocated, but it has been found that the patients suffer less with soda solution, though oil may be used if more easily obtained.

There are special directions for the handling of drowning cases, but the main thing is to keep up artificial respiration for at least two hours at the rate of twelve to the minute.

In accidents from electrical shocks, artificial respiration should also be maintained if the patient is unconscious. This should be kept up until the doctor arrives.

In cases of poisoning, anything available that will make the patient vomit should be used. Mustard water, very salty water, or quantities of lukewarm water, are usually obtainable. The doctor is, of course, notified at once in all these cases.

In epilepsy or fits, place a cloth between the teeth and leave the patient alone. No one can do any more.

To summarize, then—

First, some one must take charge of the situation in an authoritative, careful, calm manner, arranging to get medical attention as promptly as possible, and preferably carrying the patient to the physician or to the hospital to save time.

Secondly, stop hemorrhage.

Third, allow no one to put anything next to the wound unless it is sterile, and nothing at all unless aseptic INTO the wound.

Fourth, make the patient just as comfortable as possible.

Remember, that First Aid is very simple, but is tremendously important. If these few rules are carefully and understandingly followed, the amount of good rendered is inestimable, and the number of lives saved amazing.

V

USE OF FIREARMS

In the enforcement of law and order history has shown that peace officers must sometimes use firearms. It has, therefore, become legal for any police officer to carry some sort of firearm while on duty. There is no legal restriction as to what kind of firearm. Therefore, any arm that has been used under the rules of warfare may be used by the police. This includes revolvers, pistols, rifles of all description, tanks, machine guns, Gatling guns, gas, and even artillery. This article will be limited to the discussion of the ordinary work of peace officers, and so only to the use of the revolver and the rifle.

We feel that a firearm to be effective should be of the best manufacture and large enough to do any work required. Small caliber revolvers place the peace officer at a disadvantage, as he should be fully as well armed as the criminal. The same may be said of the rifle. Nothing less than the standard of the army, which is 30.30 of high power, should be used. The rifle comes into use in rural districts in the hunting down of desperate criminals who are armed, or may be used in riot duty.

The revolver, we believe, should be at least a .38 caliber or more, of standard make, and should be carried on the outside of the uniform in the place where it can be most easily drawn. There are two reasons why the revolver should be on the outside of the uniform: First, for the psychological effect, and secondly, because in the dangerous work of enforcing the law (and there is no more dangerous every-day work) a peace officer should have as good a chance as the criminal. What good, in an emergency, is a revolver in the hip-pocket under a heavy blouse and overcoat? Certainly no criminal would handicap himself as does the average police officer.

The care of firearms is very important and there are many manuals available on this subject; therefore, it will not be discussed here.

Every peace officer should be familiar with the use of small firearms. There is only one way to become proficient, and that is by practise. Marksmanship may be natural for some but certainly it is not for all. To be a good shot is an art, just as much as to be a good violin player or piano player and requires practise. No matter how well a man may have played the piano at some time in his life, still to remain proficient he must continue his practise. It is the same in the use of firearms. Police officers should have stated times to practise, should be encouraged to do so, and competition should be stimulated by prizes or rewards. Money spent on furnishing ammunition to a police force is well spent. There is nothing that so degrades a police force in the mind of the public as to have an officer who is a very poor shot blazing away at some object and missing it. One or two poor marksmen attempting to kill a dog suffering from hydrophobia and endangering the lives of everybody about, will diminish the prestige of a police force. The common expression that the members of such and such a force "couldn't hit the side of a barn" does more to encourage the crook than any one thing I know.

There is one rule that is applicable to every police force and this is it:

Never draw a revolver in the performance of duty except for the purpose of using the weapon. In other words, if it is drawn it must be used.

A revolver or rifle should be used by a peace officer only under three conditions:

First—For the purpose of practising with the weapon.

Second—To defend his life or the life of some one or more persons.

Third—In apprehending a felon who is fleeing from arrest, and then only after every known method has been used and the officer is absolutely certain that the felon will escape. Never to be used in misdemeanor cases.

A police officer is not protected by the law and must stand trial the same as any other citizen when he uses firearms. He may have been morally right, but to face a jury he must be absolutely right in his reasons for using a weapon. A policeman should never draw a revolver in making an arrest except in the night, or in some situation where he is positively sure, and it can be proved, that his life was in danger in making the arrest.

No police officer should threaten by putting his hand upon his gun or by drawing it and flourishing it about. If it is drawn be sure that it is in self-defense, by orders from a superior who has the authority, or to catch a felon who is getting away after every other method has been used to apprehend him. Desperate characters who barricade houses, who have firearms, who are felons and who have shown that they will stop at nothing, even at the taking of life, must be handled accordingly. Should they be killed there can be no criticism by a jury. These cases are extremely rare, however.

A police officer should keep constantly in mind the three rules for the use of firearms, should think them over, study every case where they have been used, form in his mind imaginary occurrences, such as a revolver in the hands of men whom he has arrested, and figure out what he would have done should the criminal have had a gun.

So, constant practise with the firearm under instruction, developing proficiency in the care and handling of the weapon, constant thought about when to use it, will make every police officer a real factor in the maintenance of law and order in his department.

VI

RIOTS AND RIOT DUTY

Whenever three or more individuals together start disturbing the peace, it is a riot. Generally speaking, there are two types of riot. Sometimes a great gathering, having come together with peaceful intent, such as students in a college town, or a crowd watching a ball game or parade, may suddenly become boisterous and ultimately go so far as to get beyond control. This is unusual but does occur, and the possibility should be kept in mind whenever a great body of people congregates.

The second class of riot is usually industrial in character and often leads to bloodshed and destruction of property. Anything further than this as to length of time and degree of disorder may be carried on into a revolution, such as resulted in France in the latter part of the eighteenth century. Revolutions will not be considered in this lecture.

All riots are the result of lawless leadership. This is the fundamental principle underlying a riot and must be recognized in order to understand riot duty. One or more individuals are the leaders, and as long as they control the mob and encourage riotous acts the riot will continue. Therefore, the way to stop a riot is to eliminate the leaders who are encouraging and stimulating disorder.

There are but two forms of government in this world as it stands today: the administrative and the representative. By administrative we mean kings, emperors, monarchs, chiefs. By representative, we mean a government by the people, and our country is probably the best example. Our thirteen original states were originally land grants from England, administered by representatives from that government. When the states decided to break away and declare themselves free by the Declaration of Independence, a war was precipitated. Later on, a constitution was drafted and adopted which has been declared to be the greatest document of its kind ever wrought by the hand of man.

There was a question as to representation. Those states having the densest population felt they should have a larger representation than the others, but finally it was agreed to divide the representation into two houses, called a "Congress," with two representatives from each state regardless of population who should be known as "senators," forming the higher house or senate. As a compromise based on population, representatives called "congressmen" were authorized who should constitute the lower house or House of Representatives. Both senators and representatives are elected by the people. It was necessary, of course, to have a president and a vice-president. The vice-president was to be the chairman of the upper house or "Senate." Cabinet officers were appointed by the president as advisers who should be heads of bureaus of National affairs.

This same idea has been carried out in the separate states and in the administration of cities. In the states we have the governor and lieutenant-governor, senators, and assemblymen (tho the senators are according to districts rather than population), and in cities we have the mayor, common council, aldermen, etc. Even in villages, we find the president and trustees.

The senators and assemblymen in a state form the legislature and they embody the power of the state in that they make rules for conduct of the people in the state. Cities, towns, or villages receive a charter from the legislature which gives them power to makes rules of conduct pertaining to the confines of the city, town, or village. These rules are called "ordinances."

There are two forces to maintain law and order in time of riot: First the police power of the state, which is by local authority, including sheriffs and state police. Second, the military power of the state.

The civil takes precedence over the military through its power to make laws of conduct and its police power. For it must be remembered that the civil pays for the military.

When riots occur they may get so out of hand that the civil authorities are not prepared to cope with them. Then it becomes necessary to call upon the military authorities. By so doing, the state or community reverts back to feudal times in that it puts itself under a military despotism called "martial law." Our forefathers, foreseeing that should the military commander be put in charge with absolute authority under martial law he might not wish to relinquish this power, wisely made the governor of a state or the President of the United States commander-in-chief of the military and naval forces of the state or nation. Then, he as the chief executive, civil in character, could command the removal of military authority at the proper time.

It is well to note that should there be rioting or disorder in a state, the federal authorities or United States government can not stop this rioting. It must be handled by the state's own power with one exception. If, for example, the democratic or republican party be in power and the opposite party, headed by leaders, should start rioting and disorder in the state, the governor would be empowered to use every available civil and military agent to suppress the rioting, and citizens could aid, for every one has the inalienable right to protect himself against insurrections and rioting and loss of property. But if the governor's forces (the state's) are not able to handle the matter he would be empowered to ask the federal government to send him aid. This would be intervention, and is sometimes sought, as in the railroad rioting at Chicago and lately in West Virginia. But the federal government can only send in troops at the request of the chief executive of the state.

Should the President of the United States send in federal troops without the request of the governor or chief executive of a state it would mean an invasion of the state by the federal government, which literally interpreted means "war." Each state must handle its own riot and disorder, asking for aid if necessary, or be at war with the federal government.

The principles of civil government are not well understood. Hence this brief résumé. In the handling of riots we will confine ourselves now to the duties of the police. Two principles are essential:

First—Strict neutrality.

Second—Elimination of the leaders.

We have found in our experience, which has been considerable in New York State, that the first thing to do is to take an estimate of the situation, remembering that the police force is an organized force as against a disorganized force or mob. The police also have the right on their side as well as organization.

The temper of the public must be considered, for after all no laws or law enforcement can ultimately amount to anything without the consent of the governed. In some cases, temporarily, the public may be in sympathy with the rioters. If this is true, extreme caution and care must be exercised by the police, for the situation is very delicate. Everything must be done strictly according to the legal custom and procedure. No mistakes can be made. Only those who are absolutely breaking the law should be arrested, witnesses must be obtained, the evidence must be safeguarded, and the matter handed over for the courts to decide.

On the other hand, should the public become tired of the rioting and disorder, and the public temperament be decidedly against the lawless element, other methods may be used, employing such forces as is necessary with extreme care in order to cause as little personal injury as possible.

Talk is cheap. The holding of meetings should not be stopped, neither should meetings, while in progress, be broken up. One or two policemen in uniform should be present, and after the meeting is over, if any one of the speakers have made seditious or anarchistic statements, he can easily be arrested and brought to justice. We believe that meetings should be allowed as long as they are orderly. Sometimes those who attend may say "How foolish the whole thing is." To stop these meetings produces a *casus belli,* or reason for rioting.

When a perfectly peaceful gathering suddenly becomes a rioting and lawless body as a result of inflammatory statements or other causes, all persons present, even tho not in sympathy with the riot, are considered as part of it and if they stay among the rioters just as sightseers they are considered a part of the mob and must suffer the consequences. Curious people do not seem to realize this fact, and try to make trouble later for the agents who are maintaining law and order if they have been made to move or have been ordered away, but sightseers must take the consequences if they will expose themselves. Sightseers are not tagged and officers can not separate them in the mob. The best rule, therefore, is for all innocent people to get away as soon as possible and keep away whenever a riot starts and continues.

Corporations which hire armed deputies should not be allowed to have these deputies off their property, which they have a right to protect, but such deputies have no authority to interfere with citizens outside of their own preserves. We have found this to be an absolutely good rule. Picketing is not unlawful at present: neither is striking in labor disputes, but it is well to let the leaders know that certain streets must be kept open for the use of the public, and cooperate for this purpose. It is well to keep those who are picketing on the move and, of course, stop at once by arrest or otherwise any violence on the part of one or more of those who are picketing, but only arrest those who are breaking the law. Should the mob be drunk with passion and on destruction bent, drastic methods will have to be used and in such a case the following procedure is advised:

Large riots practically never occur in small communities; usually in places where there are streets and houses. Whenever there is a mob you will find at the head of this mob the leaders. The most daring are there and those who are the most weak-minded are in the rear. Firmness and decision are necessary on the part of police or military leader. Never threaten. Always announce in a clear voice what you expect to do and then do it. Never draw firearms to threaten. Never shoot over the heads of a mob; it will precipitate trouble. After every other method has been used, and firearms become necessary, use them and use them properly. This is a last resort, but sometimes unavoidable. A show of force in front with a flanking movement at the same time in the rear of the mob where the weakest minds are, may disintegrate the crowd. This can be used as a surprize movement and is well worth trying. Should a panic be started in the rear and some of the mob start to run, they will be followed immediately, because a mob is like a flock of sheep and as soon as the leaders find they are not backed up but are standing alone, they will run to cover.

Where there are women (and by the way, women are most difficult to handle, for they will sometimes use red pepper, ammonia, clubs, stones), the use of the horse is invaluable. Women are instinctively afraid of horses and will run before the horsemen reach them.

In patrolling it is well to keep everybody on the move. Allow no congregating on street corners, and patrolmen should walk close to the side of buildings so that nothing can be dropped on them from above. Horsemen, too, should hug the buildings, riding on the sidewalk. This is a very essential rule. If there are snipers in buildings with guns and bombs, police sharpshooters on the opposite side of the street should walk along, keeping careful observation of windows and roofs, with the idea of shooting to kill. It may be necessary to send sharp-shooters up on the roofs of buildings.

A reserve should be kept at all times with a carefully arranged system of information by telephone or otherwise communicating with them, so that more men may be thrown into certain locations, if necessary. This reserve should be motorized and ready for instant call. The commander should establish himself with the reserves.

The club and the horse are the best means of stopping riot. One man on horseback is worth ten on foot. It is probably the most dangerous and arduous duty that any human being could be called upon to do, is this riot duty. A policeman must have self-control, must be willing to stand insulting remarks, must keep his temper, must never flinch, must never give an order unless he means it, and if he gives an order and it is disobeyed he must see that it is carried out or take the consequences. A policeman should never act on the spur of the moment, but when he does act he must act fearlessly and to the point. If force is necessary in making an arrest or in moving the rioters, striking a rioter should be avoided unless necessary, but if it is necessary the blow should fall on the body rather than on the head. A well-organized police force can go through rioting and disorder without bloodshed. A disorganized, slovenly force will aid a riot rather than diminish it, and there is usually bloodshed where there is a weak or poorly trained force.

I know of no duty that calls for greater self-control, better leadership, more common sense, than the proper handling of riots and disorder. The subject is so vast that only hints may be given in this brief lecture, but these few rules have proved of practical value and will make a good basis for successful control of a disorganized mob.

VII

TOUCHING ON FINGER-PRINTING

The New York State School for Police is not teaching the Bertillon System nor finger-printing for the following reasons:

This country with its heterogeneous population has no record of its citizens that is of real value to the police. In England there are approximately between two and three per cent foreign-born, while in this country it is variously estimated that there are from forty up to, in some localities, seventy per cent of foreigners. There is no record made of our floating population, and citizens are only known through property they own or by length of residence in a location. The record of deaths and of births is now being bettered throughout the country, and the census has its use, but unfortunately very few criminals get into the census.

At present the Bertillon system of measurements is too complicated and would require too much money to be generally used in this country.

Finger-printing, to be of general use, would have to be on such a vast scale that until a complete census and record of our population are made it seems that this method of identification can never take the position that it should hold.

In large centers like New York City, Chicago, and other great cities, habitual criminals can be finger-printed and here of course it is of advantage and specialists can be developed. Finger-print work is special work and is only an accessory in identification. It must obviously be the work of specialists, for to be of value it must be well done, just as the examination of specimens for diagnosis in the medical profession to have any value must be made by those who are specially trained and competent. In schooling of peace officers the general principles of every-day patrol work, witness work, and an understanding of the law is essential, but finger-printing to be effective must be in the hands of experts and can not be used in general unless we have a complete record of the individuals that make up our vast country.

VIII

COMPLAINTS AND REPORTS

This chapter treats of two important things: First, how to take a complaint or secure information regarding it, and, second, intelligent reports, how they should be written and what they should contain.

I

In receiving a complaint over the telephone you must be brief, secure the pertinent facts without unnecessary delay, and make your questions distinct and right to the point. Of the complaint, you must secure full particulars, without inquiring into unimportant details, getting the full name of the complainant, a complete address, that is, the county, the township, the village, the name of the road the complainant lives on, the distance from the nearest village, and the telephone number, or in cities, the street and house number. If in a tenement, the floor. This full information is absolutely necessary so that the officer in charge may know just where to send the patrol assigned to the case, and so that there may be no delays caused by insufficient or improper information. Again, if the location is in a county not covered by patrols from barracks, that is, say fifty miles from the barracks, it

would be necessary for the officer in charge to assign
one of the county patrols to the case, and unless he had
full directions in front of him he might notify a patrol
which was not as near the location as another patrol
might be. The following illustration will show how
this error might happen: Frank H. Jones telephones
to the Batavia barracks that his barn was broken into
during the night and his automobile stolen. He lives
in a little village of 150 people in Cattaraugus county,
eighty miles from Batavia. His village is not large
enough to have a telephone exchange and the "central" is located in a village 15 miles from complainant's
home. If the trooper is not particular about inquiring
as to Mr. Jones's exact location, and reports to the
officer in charge the address of the village where the
"central" is located, the officer might notify the patrol
stationed near that "central" village, whereas on that
very day there might be another patrol passing within
a mile or so of Mr. Jones's hamlet, but, the officer not
having the full and correct address, has notified a patrol
at some distance from the scene of the burglary. You
can appreciate the delay that would be caused by this,
and it might result in loss of all chance to apprehend
the culprits. This situation might also obtain in out-
skirts of cities or towns having a small police force.

Be particular when receiving a complaint to ascertain the exact nature of the crime. When a citizen calls
for the police, he always wants them immediately. In
serious cases, of course, he should have them at once,
even tho it is necessary to go to some expense to get

assistance to him. In other cases, however, of a minor nature, such as family disputes, quarrels with neighbors, etc., a police department would not be justified in spending a considerable sum of money in an effort to get officers to the complainant in haste, and, many times, it is better that they should not get there too soon, as often these misunderstandings are all patched up by the disputants after the heat of passion has subsided. Therefore, be particular to learn just what the trouble is so that the officer in charge may know how to proceed in assigning officers to the case. This is necessary, too, in deciding just what particular men to assign to the case, for if it is a very complicated case requiring the work of a man of wide experience the officer would not want to send a less experienced man to it.

If the complaint be in relation to missing persons, lost property, lost or strayed animals, etc., you must secure a full description, and every particular in connection with the person, relatives, friends, habits, peculiarities, etc., and, in the case of property and animals, every point which would assist in identification.

Again, in the case of a crime, it is well to inquire if the complainant suspects any particular person. This is of great help to police in solving crimes. We find that in small communities, the character, habits, shortcomings, virtues, etc., of every person are known to every other person in that community, so that if a crime is committed in such a locality by "local talent" the villagers can generally guess who is the culprit. Police perhaps, not residents of the section, do not know these ne'er-do-wells, and unless they inquire regarding them may miss the criminal in their investigation.

What I have said has particular reference to receiving a complaint over the telephone, or, in receiving it verbally at some point other than the place where offense was committed. Of course, if you were right on the ground, you would immediately start on the investigation.

In taking the complaint, however, it would be well to inquire if the complainant has notified the sheriff and his town constable; also, inquire as to strange and suspicious persons around the vicinity, automobiles which do not belong in that section, leaving time of trains, etc.

II

Reports should be submitted according to the standard military form, i. e., location and date in the upper-right-hand corner; then on the left, "Subject" and "To."

Each paragraph should be numbered and it should deal with one particular phase of the report. In other words, two or more subject-matters should not be dealt with in the same paragraph.

Reports should be concise, clear, and to the point, omitting unnecessary details which have no bearing on the case.

In reports written in longhand, you should print all proper names, that is, names of complainants, witnesses, informants, defendants, etc., with complete addresses, and their names should be in *full,* first name, middle initial or initials, and last name. This printing is absolutely necessary; errors are very frequently made by clerks in deciphering proper names written in longhand.

For rural police, daily patrol reports should show the names of the villages you left in the morning and arrived at in the evening, with time of departure and arrival; the names of every village you passed through during the day, no matter how small or unimportant that village may seem to you; the correct mileage for the day and whether by horse, automobile, motorcycle, train, trolley or foot; and the villages where you expect to spend the nights 24 and 48 hours hence. You should be very particular in showing these villages, and if for any police reason you do not reach them, you must notify the telephone operator where you are. The reason for this is very plain. Suppose the barracks office wants to reach you by telephone in the middle of the night on a very important case. The officer in charge gets from the file your latest patrol report and calls up the village where you have previously reported you would spend that night. You are not there; the operator does not know where you are; says you have not reported in to her. How is the officer in charge going to get you on the telephone? It is an important case. Look at the damage that is resulting from your neglect and carelessness! Stop in the postoffice and every general store and inquire as to conditions in the vicinity.

Have your patrol report stamped by the postmaster, and, if it is Sunday, have it stamped by the ticket agent at the railroad depot. If troopers are needed in that section, he can tell you in the absence of the postmaster or general storekeeper.

Arrest Reports must contain all particulars in connection with the arrest. Full name of defendant, address, age, color, time of crime and time of arrest, full and correct name of magistrate, his address, township and county, disposition of the case, etc. You should also ascertain the previous criminal history of the defendant, as magistrates must take this into consideration when passing sentence on such a person. Furthermore, department records should contain as complete a record of the "past performances" of defendants and criminals as it is possible to get. The reason for this is self-evident to any thinking person.

Reports on automobile accidents must show, as stated above, full names and addresses of principals and witnesses, license and engine numbers of the automobiles, make and style of the cars, direction in which they were proceeding, the rates of speed at which they were traveling, whether either one or both of them were violating any provisions of law, and full information showing just how the accident occurred. Who was responsible for the accident? In 99 out of every 100 automobile accident cases investigated, it is shown that some person violated the law, was careless, or did something he should not have done, which resulted in the accident. Show this conclusion in your report. With every such report you should give a diagram showing the road, the accident, position of the cars, directions, etc. You should also show in the report the condition of the road at the place where the accident happened, condition of guard-rails, culverts, bridges, etc., location of warning signs, etc. This information is essential in case an automobilist should start a civil suit against the city, county or state, alleging that the bad condition of the road or some portion of it was responsible for the accident.

Special reports should be rendered on all bad and dangerous highway conditions, broken guard-rails, damaged bridges and culverts, etc. This in order that the Highway Department may be notified and the bad features corrected, thus possibly avoiding serious accident and resulting suit against the city, county or state.

In your search for data for your reports, local newspaper offices are very helpful. These newspapers have a correspondent in every village and hamlet, who find out about everything that is going on. They report to their editors full particulars of every incident, and if this incident happens to be a crime, very often their reports will show just who is responsible. Full information, of course, is not published by the paper for fear of a libel suit, but if you are friendly to the owners of these papers, and approach them in the proper manner, you will be surprised at all the data they can give you, and will give you if they have confidence in you. Clip from the local newspapers articles on cases in which the department is interested and attach such clippings to your reports.

On very important cases, your commanding officer will require that you telephone your reports, rather than subject them to the delay of the mails. Before going to the telephone to make such a report, first be sure that you have all the information, names, addresses, etc., before you so that you can make a complete and sensible report.

Each policeman should have with him at all times a memorandum book, in which he should enter a summary of his report on every case he handles. This entry should show, in brief, the sum and substance of the report he is making in full, with names, addresses, dates, times, license and other numbers, witnesses. This should be retained for his own reference at a future date.

IX

TRAFFIC AND PARKING

A few years ago the problem of traffic upon the highways received very little attention from the authorities or public at large. Possibly the reason for this was that, until the advent of mechanical transport, the pressure on our roads was not sufficiently great to necessitate any serious effort to relieve it.

Of late, however, the problem has presented itself very insistently, and state, city, and town have been forced to make laws to meet the increase in motor traffic that has arisen and which is still constantly expanding.

This is foreseen by President Harding, who stated in his annual message to Congress:

"The motor-car has become an indispensable instrument in our political, social, and industrial life."

It is well to understand the ideal which should be striven for in handling traffic. This is: "Speed without offense." In other words every one must be permitted to get over the ground as quickly as possible without being a nuisance or menace to others.

The volume of merchandise, the number of people in transit daily over our roads, are forces that can not be left unregulated, as shown by the report of the legislative committee, headed by Senator Lowman, which investigated the automobile accidents in this state for the year past. Their findings disclose the facts that 1,981 persons were killed and 60,000 injured, to say nothing of the vast amount of money lost by this destruction of property.

Therefore, it is one of the most important duties of law enforcers to reduce these casualties by causing the motor-traveling public to conform to the state and local laws pertaining to the safe and proper use of the highways. The work known as traffic duty should be handled by police in such a courteous, efficient, and intelligent manner that motorists will declare such policing indispensable. The past has proved beyond a shadow of a doubt that the policeman who is a *traffic regulator* on the highways must also be a *traffic educator* as well. To eliminate preventable accidents, we must get down to the cause, which is that often the driver does not understand the A-B-C of motoring.

Always Be Careful. What an excellent thing it would be if this rule could be universally observed by all who drive automobiles, particularly those who have passengers relying for their safety on the operator's care and good judgment! It should be indelibly impressed upon the minds of the traveling public.

Our highway and traffic laws are based upon the rules of reason, and a strict compliance with them is absolutely necessary for the pleasure and safety of all. The task of successfully putting over this important educational propaganda is a huge one, but persistent and continuous work on the part of all policemen can not fail to bring about satisfactory results.

There are times and places where friendly warnings are of no avail, and other methods must be used to drive the wilful violators off the roads and put sense into the heads of the careless. Take, for example, the traffic conditions in the territory surrounding New York City. In addition to the regular tourist and commercial traffic we find that for a day or so prior to holidays and Sundays, when the travel is much augmented, motorists roll outward bound from the city in a fairly law-abiding manner, with of course the usual exceptions of the few drivers who seem to think that all law and order cease the moment they pass the city limits, and immediately have an attack of so-called "gasoline insanity."

These few deliberate lawbreakers are best handled by motorcycle officers. As the holiday or week-end draws to a close, the tide of traffic changes and thousands of cars travel homeward in the direction of the city. The main state roads become congested to their fullest capacity, an intolerable nerve-racking close-order march starts, orderly conditions often cease entirely, with the result that the wrecking crews find plenty to do. On certain stretches of roads, jams and accidents occur with such startling frequency that the police are forced to stamp out these evils by use of the fixed post. Two or more policemen or dismounted troopers should station themselves on a well-known danger spot, such as a blind curve, and will find that with great frequency a

Mr. Fool Killer driving a heavy car, often filled with children, will come around the curve at a high rate of speed racing abreast of the regular line of traffic regardless of the danger of hitting any oncoming car.

This is the type of casualty causer that unless cured will kill, so the trooper will step into the center of the road, blow a short sharp blast on a whistle and hold his arm extended over his head with the palm facing the oncoming car. This is the universal signal of STOP. Shouted commands should not be used, as they are often misunderstood or misconstrued into something the driver could very properly take offense at. As the car comes to a halt inform the driver that you are a state trooper, wait for an opening in the line of traffic, or if continuous, hold it up for a moment and then direct the driver to pull well over to the right side of the road and in this case you should say: "I am going to give you a summons for reckless driving. Let me see your owner's or chauffeur's card." While the law of New York State does not compel an owner, or person to whom he has loaned his car, to carry a card, such as in many other states, it is well to make him identify himself properly, altho you can not force him to do so should he decline; but under ordinary circumstances a few tactful suggestions will usually bring forth proper identification in the way of letters or cards. Fill in the body of the summons and on the back of the stub mark place and manner of violation, direction of travel, and kind of vehicle, as it is practically impossible for any policeman to remember all the details when a large number of arrests are made, and so successfully meet cross-examination of an attorney should the case go to trial.

Should the driver of the car you are attempting to stop for a traffic violation fail to comply with your signal and run by, do not commandeer a following car and start a Keystone Comedy pursuit, or under any circumstances fire your gun in the direction of the fugitive, as both these acts are absolutely wrong. Make it a practise to read and remember license numbers at a glance so that you can trace the owner of the fugitive car, get a warrant, or as a last resort obtain an investigation subpena whereby he can be made to disclose the driver's identity. The one possible exception which will permit you to pursue a fleeing car is where the driver attempts to escape from the scene of a serious or fatal accident.

In handing out a summons, it must be borne in mind that a summons is only an invitation to come to court and failure to comply carries no legal penalty with it. In case a driver does not appear at the time or place specified, the proper procedure is to lay information, obtain a warrant and go after your man if he resides in your territory. Should he live in a distant part of the state, forward the warrant to your troop headquarters where it will be passed on to the station which polices the district where the violator lives. He should be located, arrested, and forced to give bail for appearance before the magistrate who issued the warrant.

Once your mind is made up to hand out a summons, obtain the necessary information in a military man-

ner, accurately fill in the summons as rapidly as possible
and hand it to the *driver,* who should be then signaled
to proceed. If the driver states that it will be impossible or a very serious inconvenience for him to appear
on the date or at the time you have placed on the summons, offering a bona fide reason, and expresses his
willingness to appear on some future date, do not be
arbitrary but use good judgment and comply with the
request. With out-of-state drivers who are not likely to
answer a summons and for those motorists who reside
several hundred miles away, endeavor to take them before a justice immediately for an arraignment so as not
to cause an unreasonable hardship.

It will be found that a short tour of active duty at
a certain danger spot will render it comparatively safe
for some time, and when this result has been accomplished shift to another point along the road so that the
persistently reckless driver will be at a loss to discover
your whereabouts and naturally not wanting to get
arrested again will ease up on the school-crossings, sharp
turns and bad road intersections. The newspapers will
give notice of your activities on such and such roads,
auto clubs will inform their members, and motorists will
pass the word along to one another, so that in a very
short time the "don't care" idea changes to the "always be careful" one and the result will be that the
number of accidents drop to a minimum.

When presenting your traffic cases in court do so
without comment other than the actual facts necessary
for the magistrate's information. Long-winded pleas

for a conviction are not good policy, as such action is very apt to make a bad impression on the mind of the court, possibly conveying the idea that you are over-zealous in the matter of prosecution. Make your testimony convincing by its fairness and accuracy.

Your complaints and statements regarding reckless driving should always be based upon the *manner of operation* and not upon the rate of speed. There is a popular misconception about the dangers of traveling fast. As a matter of fact most automobile accidents occur independently of speed, and are due more to carelessness, recklessness or incompetent driving than to the actual rate of travel.

Some of the worst accidents happen to slow-moving cars, for which reason legislative interdiction of speed by no means precludes the possibilities of mishap. We must endeavor to ascertain whether we have a case of reckless driving, or merely a driver in a hurry to get somewhere quickly but safely. Thus, we often make arrests when motorists are driving comparatively slowly and approve other cases where drivers are traveling at the rate of 40 miles per hour. It isn't the speed alone that counts; it's the speed plus the conditions.

Under Section 14, Chapter 70 of the Consolidated Laws of New York, which is the General Highway Traffic Law, the definition states: "That reckless driving for the purpose of this chapter shall include driving or using a vehicle, etc., in a manner which *unnecessarily endangers* users of the highway, or *unnecessarily interferes* with the free and proper use of the highway." You will notice that no mention of speed is made so you should refrain from such statements as "Defendant was traveling 40, 50 or 60 miles an hour." In the case of the People vs. Winston, 155 N. Y. App. Div., the decision states: "So, an information based solely on driving . . . more than 30 miles an hour should allege that the excessive speed was maintained for one-quarter of a mile, and *that fact should be proved.*" Eliminate the rate of speed from your testimony, as a clever lawyer can generally disprove your assertions on this point. The fact that the defendant was *unnecessarily endangering* the users of the highway will suffice. Slowly but surely our courts are responding to the popular clamor to make the highways safe, by convicting and properly punishing guilty traffic offenders, so that in the future we can feel assured of a stronger spirit of cooperation between the courts of special sessions and police in carrying out the mandates of the law.

In regulating traffic on fixed post make your hand signals so clear-cut as to preclude any chance of being misunderstood. A whistle is of material aid, as city motorists are generally more on the alert for whistle rather than voice signals. Under no circumstances ever attempt to direct traffic by waving your club, as there is a case on record where a trooper in motioning to a driver with his riot-stick was reported. The complainant being a well-meaning but somewhat excitable individual insisted that the trooper was shaking the club at him in a threatening manner. So, should you be on post and not have your holder, simply shorten the rawhide thong and slip it over your revolver butt or under the left-hand pocket button of your blouse. It is imperative that a policeman on traffic duty keep himself, uniform, and equipment policed up to the nth degree of military neatness, as he is often the subject of considerable attention from travelers who gage the entire department from the appearance of a single man. Tourists and others will ask directions, distances to certain points and other information so that it is quite necessary for you to study up on your territory in order to give a prompt, intelligent answer that will reflect the alertness of the department, as any moron can say, "I don't know," when asked a simple question.

Occasionally, troopers will be called upon to block a road over which some fugitive criminal is endeavoring to escape, and in these cases it is well to take advantage of some sharp right angle turn where the car will have to slow down. Let your partner stand about fifty yards beyond you when you signal for the vehicle to stop, and it will be found that the crook who might take a chance in running by you will refrain from this act because of the presence of the second trooper up the road.

Care must be exercised in stopping cars driven by lawbreakers especially in these bootlegging times, for only a short time ago in northern New Jersey three police officers were deliberately run down and very seriously injured by an individual who was endeavoring to make his getaway after the commission of a crime.

For the motor-cycle man who may be forced to pursue a motor vehicle traveling at a high rate of speed, be careful in your manner of approach, for it is known that criminally inclined drivers have deliberately and maliciously swerved their cars so as to injure the officer seriously.

When you find traffic congested or halted there is always a reason, and it is up to you to find out promptly the cause and remove it. Wrecks that block the road should be immediately ditched, for by the use of a fence rail or post as a lever and a few volunteers even the heaviest car can be manhandled out of the way. Simple-minded truck drivers who "hog" the highway and for various reasons take up a greater portion of the road when halted should be taught where they belong.

During the last few summers pedlers of various kinds of refreshments have been making themselves more or less of a nuisance by attracting motorists who park in front of their stands, thereby blocking the road. However, by explaining the penalty attached to Article 148, Section 1530, Penal Laws, you will cause these offenders to provide the necessary parking space so as to keep the road clear.

Be careful to hold up traffic when a vehicle catches fire on the highway and is beyond saving, as an explosion is likely to occur when the flames reach the gas tank.

On washouts, broken bridges, etc., throw up a temporary barricade and arrange for a detour as quickly as possible. Wind storms will sometimes cause a heavy tree to fall across the road, but a saw or ax borrowed from the nearest farmhouse and a little exercise will soon remove the obstacle. The clearing up of unforeseen and unusual blockades will depend in a large degree on your ingenuity and no fixed rule can be laid down except that you *must* keep the roads open and traffic rolling along.

At a scene of a serious accident three things should be carried out in the following order:

First: Detain the party responsible for the accident, especially if a fatal outcome is probably pending the coroner's action.

Second: Secure prompt medical attention for the injured.

Third: Clear the road without delay.

When the crash has resulted in an immediate death, arrest the driver or drivers.

Do not touch the body, but promptly notify the coroner and remain on guard until that official arrives.

The old Gilbertian refrain, "A policeman's life is not a happy one," must have originated in the brain of some ex-traffic officer, for there are many times when the proper enforcing of the law creates decidedly disagreeable situations. Take, for example, a few of the unpleasant types that an officer regulating traffic on the road will encounter in the day's work. There are the arrogant persons who labor under the hallucination that they are above the law by reason of some fancied importance, who attempt to intimidate an officer who stops them for a traffic violation by threatening to have him removed. As this is a violation of section 1824 of the Penal Law, inform the offender that you may make an additional arrest for threatening an officer in the performance of his duty. This usually has a calming effect.

Pugilistic truck chauffeurs who desire to demonstrate their talent when summoned should be promptly placed under arrest and charged with disorderly conduct. Delightful young lady traffic offenders will attempt to smile their way past the dreaded summons book, and jovial citizens often imagine that a hearty laugh will cover up their violating some rule of the road. Scoundrels occasionally make the mistake of attempting to bribe some officer who apprehends them for a traffic offense. These smiles and frowns, like the sunshine and rain, must be encountered and withstood in the impersonal and gentlemanly manner which is expected of a trained police officer.

During the summer months there is an ever-growing demand for troopers to handle traffic at country races, carnivals and fairs. People have found out through bitter experience that their day's pleasure has often been entirely spoiled by the chaotic traffic conditions that exist when these events are not properly policed. The ununiformed rural constable, often just hired for the day, is generally more of a hindrance than help, as he has a weird and wonderful idea regarding the parking of cars. His theory is to jam as many vehicles as possible in a given parking space regardless of system. The result of his handiwork may be seen when some motorist who has the misfortune to be wedged in the center of the mass of cars attempts to leave ahead of the rest.

When the Department of State Police took over this phase of traffic work it made a thorough study of the various methods in vogue at the time, and reached the conclusion that none were satisfactory. A new plan called the "Herring-Bone System" was then evolved and experts consider it the best in the traffic world to-day. By its use a systematic and orderly plan of parking thousands of cars can be obtained without accident, delay or confusion.

While of course the practical application of this method will vary with the shape and size of the space available for parking purposes and number of cars expected, a study of the appended diagram will make the principle clear.

The incoming cars to be parked enter a single gate and follow a one-way road as shown by the arrow, proceed up to the top of the field where they turn, coming down, parking alternately left and right, back to back, on the edge of the road until the column is full when another row is started, thereby forming an orderly block of cars from which any vehicle can be immediately removed.

In a very large gathering, enough officers should be present to allow the filling of several columns at the same time. At the New York State Fair many thousands of cars are parked by this method without confusion.

For parking cars in those communities which have

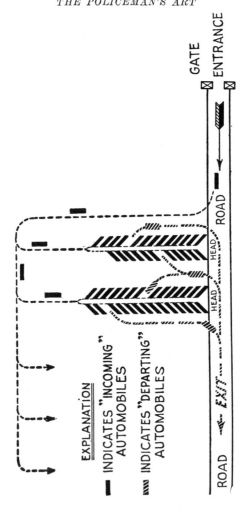

THE HERRING-BONE SYSTEM OF PARKING.

allotted proper space on the main thoroughfares, the most satisfactory and safe system is to have the vehicle *back* into the curb at a 45 degree angle headed with and not against the line of traffic. After the cars have been properly parked and vacated by the occupants, the police should remain on guard in the vicinity to deter any criminally inclined person from performing unlawful acts against the property entrusted to their care. On holidays and other occasions where large bodies of motorists gather for some event, due allowance must be made for the holiday spirit and under no circumstances should any person's feelings be offended by a traffic officer assuming an arbitrary manner. Officers should see that members of their detail maintain a cheerful attitude, as a surly officer is generally an incompetent one.

For petty violations always use discretion and do not be too technical, as a warning sometimes has just as much effect as an arrest. There are occasions when even the most careful motorist will unconsciously or unwittingly become a lawbreaker. Tail-lights will go out without the knowledge of the driver, dust and mud make license plates unreadable, headlights will burn out between garages and the fully equipped driver will find that his spare lamps have been broken in the tool box.

Doctors sometimes responding to an emergency sick call will take chances which they would not under normal conditions. A motorist will dash ahead to warn some car that the brakes are on fire. These are just examples of where a policeman should use good judgment. Inform the violator that he has broken the law, but do not attempt to deliver any long-winded discourse on it. Simply and briefly state the violation and· if he offers a reasonable excuse, permit him to proceed on his way, but if he is antagonistic use your last resort, a summons, or immediate arrest.

Remember that our prime duty is sensibly to expedite traffic and not retard it, and that we must make allowance for the fact that altho over 90 per cent of the motorists are doing the best they can, some will just happen to slip over the border line into the realm of the technically guilty. Always give the driver the benefit of the doubt and never lose sight of the fact that police should maintain a *courteous* and *common-sense enforcement of the law.* In other words *"Say it with a smile."*

X

TELEPHONE COURTESY

The importance of courtesy over the telephone is not generally understood. A public servant more than any one else should know the value of an impression gained from a telephone conversation.

You are the agents, the representatives of a public department. By your manner, your department, and, incidentally, your city or state is judged. If you were sent in person as a messenger by the governor of this state, you would take heed to look your best, and to conduct yourself in such a way as to make the very best impression.

Every organization rises or falls on the impression made by its representatives.

Governments, labor-unions, societies and organizations of all kinds try to send out those who will create the best impression, and through that impression gain the best results for themselves. Sometimes you read of an ambassador who is returned to his own country on account of not being acceptable, thereby placing his government in an embarrassing position.

Personal appearance is of course negative in a telephone conversation, so that a pleasing personality or good looks have no bearing in the impression made over the wire.

It is by the ear alone that the speaker is judged. How important then is the voice, the tone, and the courteous manner! The telephone companies themselves know this fact well, and their employees are taught to speak politely and never to show irritation. We are all familiar with the pleasant words: "Excuse it, please," and "I beg your pardon," with which "central" is instructed to meet a peevish complaint. She may feel irritable herself, but she is not allowed to show it.

The secret of a successful telephone conversation, therefore, is prompt service and a courteous manner. It is not so much the ultimate success of the undertaking as it is the manner in which the task is accepted and the willingness shown to be of service.

A policeman answering the telephone should have in mind that he is a public servant and should try and give even a little more than is asked for.

When a policeman answers the telephone he should immediately state his location and name, for example: "Officer Brown, 25th Precinct Station." If inquiry is made for the captain, the answer should be "I will get him at once," or if he is not there advise the name of the officer in charge. The party concerned is generally so favorably impressed by such intelligence in answering that he goes no further but decides that here is a man competent to handle his case. This not only redounds to the credit of the department, but is sometimes discussed with the department head and may mean advancement for the officer who answered the call.

How different is the impression made by the officer who picks up the telephone and starts off by saying "Who's this? The captain ain't here," and other curt answers of this kind which are so common in telephone conversations. The party concerned immediately loses confidence in the officer talking, and by the time he succeeds in getting the man he wants on the wire is in a fighting mood, as he probably thought his business the most important in the world and deserving of the greatest consideration.

Barking out the question "Who's this?" at the very start of a conversation is probably the most irritating thing that ever comes over the wire. It rouses instant antagonism at the other end. Particularly is this so when the one who put in the call begins that way.

If you are calling, remember that you have chosen a time that is convenient to you, and it may not be at all so to the person at the other end. You can not be too considerate, then.

If you rang a man's doorbell, and wanted to see him on business, you would certainly not snap at the person who opened the door, "Who are you?" Yet this same thing is done every day over the wire.

Give your own name, then, before it is asked, and in case the party who calls does not give his, ask pleasantly, "Who is this, please?" or "Will you tell me who is speaking, please?"

Giving service on the telephone is just as much of an art as your other police work, and is well worth the study and attention of all police officers, particularly those who aspire to be advanced in rank. Show a vital interest in the case at hand; if the complainant is irritable, win his good graces by not getting excited with him. Offer every assistance within your power, but do not make rash promises of what you will do, as it is better to promise nothing and accomplish a little, than to promise much and accomplish nothing.

With much of the world's business being done over the telephone, the time is fast approaching when incompetency on the telephone will not be tolerated in public servants.

It should be every one's endeavor, in whatever position in life, to cultivate the same courtesy over the telephone that one renders in a personal interview.

XI

POLICE AND THE PRESS

This paper is not addressed by a metropolitan jour-
nalist to metropolitan policemen. It is an effort by a
newspaper man from the foot of Main Street to bring
to the attention of the coming Main Street policeman
ways in which mutual respect and understanding will
enable these two Main Street forces to cooperate in
the work of keeping Main Street traffic moving.

To a greater extent than you may think, we confront
the same problems. Just as there are many persons
who think a policeman's chief work should be to club
those whom they (the "thinkers") do not like, or dis-
guise themselves as haystacks and follow "clues," so there
are many and noisy persons who think a newspaper's
principal function should be to verbally club their political, social or business rivals, or to scent out "sensations." Too many policemen and newspapers of the
wrong kind have, by their conduct and declarations,
lent color to these erroneous notions. I am writing of
policemen and newspapers of the right kind—decent,
thoughtful, and efficient.

Both are appealed to by reasonable and unreasonable
persons to do things that ought to be done and that
ought not to be done. Both must be able to discrim-

inate, quickly, accurately, and, with what politeness
and diplomacy they are able to command, deal with demands that should not be acceded to in such a way as
to make as few enemies as possible. Both must be prepared to meet emergencies, to deal with the unexpected,
to mix in the affairs of other people, and both must
expect to be misunderstood very often by those in whose
affairs they have become involved. Why shouldn't
they try to understand one another, to work together,
especially as understanding and cooperation are vital
to the success of both?

The newspaper man must earn his pay by doing his
work under the keenest competition. News is the most
perishable of products. It must be found, written,
printed, circulated, in a very few hours. From the raw
material of the world's happenings, over which he has
no control and which occur in ever-varying volume,
without warning, without program or order, the newspaper man must manufacture the finished product in
anywhere from a few hours to a few seconds after the
raw material has come into existence, and do it in a way
to satisfy a multitude of critical customers. He must
be on time, he must miss nothing and he must not make
mistakes. His errors are matters of record, open to
the inspection of thousands of readers, and may be of
such a nature as to cost him his job, cost his paper
thousands of dollars in damages, or land him in prison.

Do you wonder that the reporter, especially the comparatively inexperienced one, is abrupt, nervous, in a
hurry, not always as polite as one could wish when you

do not or can not furnish him with the facts he seeks? Do you wonder that newspapers sometimes get things wrong?

For the newspaper man does not know all things. He does not know your job as well as you know it, but he does know how to find out—how to sift the few grains of truth from the bushels of chaff of street rumors and gossip. Without newspapers gossip is unrestrained, rumors grow as they spread, and it is only when the printed word appears that they are checked by the publication of the facts—often by failure to publish anything at all because there has not been a single fact on which to base the rumors.

Once the President of the United States, on his way to New England, came as far as our town in a government ship which lay in the river until he returned from his trip by rail. "The President's yacht," said a trolley-car conductor in answer to the question of a passenger. Another passenger, just alighting, overheard only the answer and didn't overhear that just right. What he thought he heard was: "The President's shot." He thought it was big news and got busy. In an hour it was all over town. It happened to be just the hour between closing the last form and delivering the papers. There was nothing in the paper about the rumor or about the President being shot. That settled it. "If it isn't in the paper it didn't happen," was the verdict of everybody.

If you ever have a big excitement in your town, you will find that the newspapers are your only reliance for

quieting it, by telling the truth, which will never be so
exciting as the false rumors that will be in circulation
between editions of the papers. But the papers must
have news, facts. How are they obtained? This is
where the police come in strong. The ideal news editor has been described as "one who knows where hell is
going to break loose next, and has a man there to see
it pop." Unfortunately no editor has yet made a perfect score on this requirement, so news must be gathered from those who happened to see events occur, or
to whom these events were reported, or whose duty it is
to investigate events of certain kinds. We must have
recourse to what we call "sources"—that is, persons
official or otherwise to whose attention certain events
will come in the regular course of duty. One of these
"sources" is the police.

News is the unusual, and so long as crime is unusual
it will be news. That is why the reporter tries to be
friendly with the police, who are the "source" from
which he obtains most news of crime. Another reason
is that a good policeman is a trained observer, and his
description of anything he has seen is much more accurate than that of the ordinary man. A good reporter
seeks, by deserving it, to gain and hold the confidence
of his "source," and with the police he succeeds unless
the policeman is not a good policeman, is inexperienced,
puffed up with importance, or a born grouch. Inexperi-
ence is curable. The swell-head and the grouch are not
likely to remain long on any police force. The reporters will see to that.

The good reporter, like the good policeman, will respect a confidence. He will be bound by it. But a gruff refusal, or a lying statement, will incite him to unusual effort to dig out and write the facts, and the policeman who tried to bluff is not likely to have a star part in the story.

If you are the right kind of policeman you will not try to have yourself written up as the hero of every tale. But sometimes you will be the hero. When you are, do not permit it to make your head swell too much. Reporters are sometimes exuberant in their praise of a policeman they like. Don't let it go to your head. Men have been spoiled by taking praise too seriously. I recall constables who happened to do a good piece of work and who were written up in a way they liked so well that they never did a stroke of work afterward, but devoted the remainder of their lives to sleuthing around and making a laughing-stock and a nuisance of themselves.

XII

POLICE AND CHARACTER

*An address delivered before the students of the New
York State School for Police*

Young men, you are fitting yourselves to enter the
field of police work, and it was for this purpose that
you have attended this school. Your efforts and the
efforts of your instructors during the past month have
been that you should enter the field with a better
knowledge of police practise than many of your older
brother officers had who have served during the years
past. It has been their aim, and I am sure it will be
yours, to devote your life service to the making of a
better world, for truly the police in a large degree influence a great many people, men, women, and children, to live better lives. The more perfect the life of
the policeman, the more perfect the organization, the
better the department can work and exert its good influence in a community.

I am glad that a training-school for policemen has
been established. In former years it was the custom
to hand a newly appointed patrolman his badge, police
rules, baton, keys, and revolver and then inform him
of the location of his post and send him out without

further instructions as to laws and ordinances or how to enforce them. Nor did he have any knowledge, other than a citizen's knowledge, of how to make an arrest. In a great many cases the new appointee would make them without proper justification and render himself liable to prosecution for false arrest; or, he would be the victim of assault by the person he attempted to arrest, unless the person submitted quietly.

To change this condition, several of the larger cities have instituted training-schools in connection with their police departments and the results have been surprizingly in favor of their continuance.

With proper training, a young policeman goes on the job with sufficient knowledge of police matters to prevent his falling into the various pitfalls which he is sooner or later to encounter in his experience.

I am sure the citizens of this State will appreciate this new venture to educate and elevate the policeman. The average citizen likes to have all the laws and ordinances properly and intelligently enforced. Then, too, he needs to have the laws explained to him and it should be one of the duties of a policeman, whenever the occasion permits, to explain laws and ordinances to citizens in order that they may have a clear understanding of them. This practise has met with approval in my city and has lessened the possibilities of arrest. Law enforcement generally does not cause any inconvenience to the average citizen who is engaged in the ordinary lawful pursuits of life, nor does he have any fear of a policeman. The law does not worry him any because it is a part of his daily life to obey the law. The good citizen is friendly to the average policeman who is endeavoring to do his duty, and he is regarded in the same manner as would be any other person engaged in any other honorable profession.

The relation between the state, city, and village police is every day becoming more closely alined. Modern methods of enforcing the laws have caused all our policemen to advance with the spirit of the times. The old method of a policeman being popular with the citizens is still in vogue, but it is applied in a different manner. Popularity does not longer indicate that a policeman *must* let the laws be violated. On the contrary, he *should* indicate his own respect for the arm of the law which he represents. The state and city police are all imbued with this advanced idea. The citizens of the state are proud of their police. There never has been a time when the policeman has been so welcome in any society as at the present. He is a personage whom all good citizens desire around. It is seldom that one hears the expression we used to hear, "A policeman is never around when he is wanted." The up-to-date system of motorizing police departments, together with the increased ambition of the modern police officer to serve the citizens, has buried this expression, I hope forever. You can imagine my surprize not very long ago, when raiding a place of bad character, to hear this expression from one of the patrons of the place who was evidently disappointed. He said, "You fellows are always around where you are not wanted." A tendency to squareness on the part of a police officer secures him more friends than he could secure in any other manner. Dealing kindly, squarely, but firmly with one's fellow citizens will soon teach those citizens that they must deal in the same manner with you.

You have learned many things during your stay here; things which will better fit you for your tasks in the future. This you must remember: "Learning itself is but little." The policeman who is *made* is an achievement, but the work of doing the things you have learned is a greater achievement. A college education is of but little use to a person if, after graduation, he does not apply it. A person who fits himself by some special training and then does not make use of that training has wasted his time. If you men fail to apply the police principles you have learned here they will be of no benefit to you. It is the practical application of the things learned which makes the surgeon, the mechanic, the artist, or any other person of talent proficient and successful.

A community expects a great deal of a police department since its members are constantly in view of the citizens, who have an excellent opportunity to study the men in uniform. The better they apply themselves to their work the more influence they have with the citizens and the more they are respected by them, and the greater the cooperation between them. In a great many respects a police force is a moral force and a greater application of this moral force is anticipated in the personnel of future policemen. Therefore, in choos-

ing the profession of a policeman you are lending your
aid to one of the greatest possible moral forces of the
country. Your opportunities for doing good will be
constant. You will daily apply the principles you have
learned here. He who applies them constantly and continuously will succeed.

Police departments up to a few years ago were considered to be only agencies for the arrest and conviction of persons who violated the law, and up to the present time only in a limited sense has the prevention of
crime been considered a part of police service. We
are beginning to realize that prevention of crime is a
more important service than conviction after the crime
has been committed, and all police departments are
considering ways of enlarging their powers to prevent
crime. Criminal problems of to-day require broad,
patriotic, humane and cooperative policies of treatment.

I have been the head of a police department for
about fourteen years and can safely say that I learned
the value of cooperation years ago when I was a lieu-
tenant of the State Militia. Three things were firmly
impressed on my mind very early in my experience;
they were patriotism, discipline and cooperation.

A patriot is one who gives his services to his country, state, or city for some worthy cause which will
benefit mankind. A million or more examples of
patriotism were evident during the recent great conflict. Discipline is necessary and must be maintained
in the home, in the school and vocational institutions,
in the office, on the street. In fact, everywhere cer-

tain rules govern the conduct of every citizen. Without discipline we would be like a ship without a rudder and would be drifting everywhere with no definite object in view. Discipline is also like the gyroscope; it steadies the ship of society and makes institutions run smoother.

Cooperation is the uniting of the mind's forces to do certain things jointly or to accomplish the same end. For instance, a police force resolves that it will unite in fighting crime or unite to raise its own general character to the highest notch. It resolves that it will aid and assist every other police department in the apprehension of criminals. It resolves that state or city shall be a respectable place to live in. It resolves that its department shall be a model police department, a department which would gain the confidence of all citizens, and it works together for all these ends. Cooperation can do great things, particularly if the object is a worthy one.

The recent World War was perhaps the most wonderful example of cooperation which could be placed before you. Here the armies of several great countries combined for a common cause. How well they succeeded in furthering the cause is a matter of history at the present time. The value of cooperation, however, can probably be demonstrated better by applying it to some of the more ordinary things we meet with in our daily life. The firemen fighting a fire must cooperate and place their streams of water in the most necessary places, and control their activities in such a manner that one will not interfere with the other. Factory employees must cooperate in executing their work so that one department or branch will not hinder or upset another, in order that the output may be steady and constant. The teachers of our schools cooperate in order that pupils may pass from one grade to another and finally graduate. Court, municipal and state officials must all cooperate so that proper government can be maintained for the benefit of the people. A police department, in order to be an effective organization, must harmonize in all respects; there must be cooperation in all its branches.

The police of the State of New York, at the present time, are sorely in need of a better spirit of cooperation in the furtherance of their work. By police I mean every police officer, whether he be a sheriff, policeman, state trooper or railway detective. There should be more harmony in police work.

Conditions throughout the State indicate the need of greater police activity. The large increase in population with the comparative lack of increase in police departments has, in fact, doubled the work. Besides the increased criminal tendencies, general use of motor vehicles and social unrest all demand more police facilities, a greater application of modern police methods and a greater spirit of cooperation among the police of different localities.

I will liken the police of this State to a large electrical unit; the heavy duty machines are in the larger cities, the lighter are distributed according to their needs in the smaller cities; and still smaller in the villages, etc. All are endowed with the same power and authority in the same way as the electrical current is standardized throughout the State. Electric current is the same in Albany as it is in New York City. It will do the same kind of work and on a smaller scale will do the identical work that is done in New York. Police forces are operated on somewhat similar lines; their work is somewhat the same in different districts throughout the State. With the unit of electricity standardized, it is possible for all electric stations to synchronize or work together, to cooperate, and being, as they are, standardized as to strength of current and other conditions, they harmonize and work together. Police departments can do the same thing if they will blend their powers and activities more closely to perform their duties, harmonize for the good and welfare of the city, cooperate for the purpose of strength. Electrical transmission is sometimes disturbed by foreign things such as "grounds," electrical storms, and other foreign currents. The activities of police departments are also sometimes disturbed by jealousies and other dangerous cross-currents. Electric stations are protected by ground-detectors and lightning-arresters, and as soon as trouble is indicated efforts are made to remedy the defects. Police forces should have their machinery so arranged and protected that jealousies and other disturbing cross-currents or elements can not mar a perfect working plan of police cooperation. A perfect organization is good to look upon, if its perfect points are visible, by reason of its activities in matters for which it was organized. Furthermore, all things are gained through harmony. Little seeds of cooperation sown in a department will grow to sturdy plants if carefully watched, and will strengthen, broaden, and elevate it.

There are in this state cooperative electrical plants, plants which take care of the villages outside the cities and which work in harmony with the city plants, thus giving rural districts all the advantages of electrical power and lighting. There is, likewise, in this state a cooperative police force, known as the State Troopers, which gives to the rural districts and villages police service of the same character and kind as is received by the citizens of the cities. This body of men was organized a few years ago for this purpose, and it has more than fulfilled its mission and is the most cooperative unit of police organization in the state. Like electricity, it is so constituted that it can, at a moment's notice, synchronize or attach itself to the units of any city in the state and be of valuable service. Police methods have advanced to such a condition that the state and city police absolutely rely upon each other in police matters. Every benefit anticipated when this body of men was organized has been realized. They are indispensable to the state and communities which they serve. They have been efficient to a high degree in proportion to their number, and if augmented would be more efficient. A greater spirit of harmony between the city and state police is urged. Each has a great duty to perform, each a certain responsibility to assume. How much better the work can be done if it be done together! Two men on a job who work together can do two full days' work, but if one pulls and the other holds nothing can be accomplished.

While there is need for more cooperation between the state, city and village police, and the official relationship between these organizations is good, a few things might bring them in closer harmony.

For instance: A broad understanding between police officials that no matter what department they belong to, they are all engaged in the same kind of work, and all are trying to accomplish the same ends—fighting crime and endeavoring to make our cities and villages respectable places to live in. What difference should it make whether you wear a blue, a gray, or an olive drab uniform! A little dynamo will work in harmony with a larger one and assume its portion of the work. Any police department should work in harmony with all other departments, in proportion to its strength.

There has always been a more or less fraternal feeling between all police officers. The reason for this, I suppose, is that one officer naturally feels a relationship toward another engaged in the same line of work. This feeling of fraternal relationship could be enlarged upon and further strengthened if all officers would express themselves a little more freely along these lines. Also, a booster or two in each department would, I believe, accomplish great results in this direction. There are several things which will, no doubt, in the near future, bring about a closer spirit of cooperation between the police of the State and its communities. This school will educate and train policemen, and by doing so will create a source of new ideas which will benefit all departments and which will establish a closer official relationship between the police officials of the State and, therefore, establish a more perfect unity of actions in all police matters.

We need a better means of communication between police departments. Lack of such proper facilities is the cause of a great deal of dissatisfaction between police departments. Police as well as citizens like speedy police service. May the practical application of the wireless telephone be hastened! I have found that if communication can be established the greatest cooperation will be possible, and in this day of rapid transit for the criminal we need to speed up our operations in this direction.

As the soldier is the unit of the army so the policeman is the unit of the police force. In order to secure the proper cooperation expected of a modern police force, the personnel of the men must be of a standard which will guarantee cooperation under the most adverse circumstances. Therefore, to my mind, man is the unit of cooperation. If this is so, then in forming police forces great care should be taken to select the right type of men for policemen.

Popular action is too often guided by feeling instead of by judgment. If one seeks a lawyer to try a case, or a physician to cure an illness, or an engineer to build a bridge, he does not make the selection with the view of rewarding some one whom he likes. He selects some one who can best do the thing that is to be done; a competent, trustworthy, skilful man. Yet, when some one was to be selected as a policeman, the old method was to select some one who was "a good fellow," or a person who needed the salary, or one who wanted the honor of the position. Popularity and not competency was the test, tho the business of being a policeman was exceedingly complicated and difficult. This job of being a policeman requires the highest quality of intelligence and character if the work is to be well done, and as the requirements of a police department grow more exacting every year, the good or bad, the effective or ineffective conduct of a police organization plays continually a greater part in the welfare, peace, and happiness of our citizens.

Scientists claim that man has three distinct natures, any one of which in its perfect state is a decided asset. They are as follows: first, the physical nature; second, the intellectual nature; third, the moral nature.

A man possessed of all these qualifications to a degree which measures up to present-day requirements, makes an excellent police officer. If he has the proper physical qualifications, which he must have, he is fitted for his task in one particular only. Physical strength alone does not meet all the requirements demanded of a policeman to-day. A man might be strong physically, strong in body, and so weak in mind that he would be totally unfit to be trusted with the duties which are a part of the daily routine of an officer of the law. Besides, with all his brawn, he might be unable to cope with the intelligent man—especially the intelligent criminal—of far less physical ability.

If the policeman possesses proper intellectual qualifications he is still further advanced toward the making of a model officer of the law. Policemen should have the advantage of a certain amount of education. They should be able to read and write the English language intelligently, and possess powers of reasoning in order that they may give proper attention to the problems which will be a part of their daily lives and duties. They should be able to converse intelligently on most of the topics of present-day activities. They should have general information regarding all professions and trades of to-day and should be able to read character to a certain extent.

In order to be a model policeman, a man must possess a moral nature. A man might be a physical and intellectual giant but if he still lacked the moral nature he would be a failure as a policeman. A policeman should be strong physically, keeping himself fit by daily exercise and temperate living. He should endeavor to improve his mind, being alert to the requirements of his position. He should endeavor to supply himself with everything necessary to give him a good working knowledge of his job, in order that he may exercise sound judgment in the performance of his duties.

He should also familiarize himself with all phases of police practise. He should set himself a certain standard of living and doing things along a high moral plane and allow nothing to turn him from his course. He should be honest and upright in his dealings with all mankind; cheerful in spirit; kind but firm in the performance of his duties. He should not be swayed by the opinions of others but should be strong enough to choose the right from the wrong course and then pursue the right course.

This moral quality of mankind appears to have been somewhat underestimated in the past when "good reputation" was frequently mistaken for "good character." Men of good reputation have sometimes failed to exhibit moral courage enough to suppress a condition which they knew to be wrong. But a man of moral nature would not permit such a condition to exist, because it would be contrary to his very nature to do so. A man with just a physical and intellectual nature might permit the wrong .condition or give it no attention because his moral nature would not let him know that the condition existed. So you see in forming a police department, these three characteristics of man should all receive consideration because they are the vital elements necessary for cooperation, harmony, and success. A poet has said:

"God give us men a time like this demands;
 Strong minds, great hearts, true faith and ready hands;
 Men whom the lust of office does not kill;
 Men whom the spoils of office cannot buy;
 Men who have opinions and a will;
 Men who have honor and will not lie;

Men who can stand before a demagog and scorn his
　treacherous flatterie without winking;
Tall men, sun-crowned, who live above the fog in pub-
　lic duty and in private thinking."

Now it might appear to you that I have set the standard for a policeman pretty high, but in fact I have not.
Our State abounds with just such men and I have reason to presume that you men have been selected because
you have exhibited many of those very traits of character necessary to qualify you for your work. Sometimes in the course of life, we forget our true nature and
it is only in tight places that it creeps out. I know of
no other work that will bring a man's character to the
front sooner than the work of a policeman.

While in the performance of your duties you will
meet all sorts of conditions and problems and sometimes
you will be sorely beset by temptations. It is then that
your true manhood will assert itself. You will find
that early in your experience you will be called upon
to decide which course you will pursue and in deciding
it will be necessary for you to call upon all your
fortitude to help you to choose the right path. Once
you have chosen, whichever way you choose, the next
time will find it easier for you to make a choice. So,
in speaking for better cooperation I urge that you
choose the way by which you can give the most and
best service. Regard your oath of office as something
sacred. Let nothing interfere with your carrying out
its mandates. Be loyal to your duty. In, and through,
and upon you rest the future police departments of

this State. A temple is no stronger than the foundation upon which it stands. Lay your foundation strong and on solid ground and your future will stand all storms.

XIII

HORSEMANSHIP

As man developed, his first achievement was his mastery of the lower animals.

The dog came first under his domination, and willingly assumed the role of companion, and has remained his true friend for centuries. Next came the horse and many other beasts of burden, such as the camel, elephant, ox, donkey, ostrich, all of which have been used in different countries as carriers for man, but among them the horse stands supreme.

Don't be dazzled by the wonders of mechanical transportation. Remember that the steam railroad runs upon tracks and must follow prescribed lines, that the automobile depends upon roads and in a measure upon weather, that tractors are expensive and are only of use in big undertakings and in highly civilized localities where mechanics are available, and supplies and equipment are easily obtainable. Such places are few in number throughout the great inhabited area of this world.

Don't forget that the horse can go where all mechanical means fail, and in all kinds of weather. He has always been and will continue to be man's surest means of transportation.

The first horses were brought to North America by the Spanish conquerors of the Southwest. Both Cortez and De Soto brought horses with them, and De Soto is known to have abandoned some of his horses in what is now Texas. These and other strays were the progenitors of the wild mustangs which were so abundant on the Western plains a century later, and which furnished the American Indians with mounts for the first time.

In rural police work, horses are an essential factor, and in cities, too, a certain number of mounted police are absolutely necessary.

A most important duty of a mounted policeman is to keep his horse in such good condition that he may do his work to the best advantage. He should make himself thoroughly acquainted with the natural history and physiology of the horse, the effects of different diseases and their treatment, and should have an intimate knowledge of his horse's endurance. It is essential that he familiarize himself with the most commonly known symptoms of diseases, and he should know something about administering medicine for such diseases. This does not mean that a mounted policeman should be a veterinary, but he should have a thorough understanding of his mount.

The horse requires gentle treatment, and persistent kindness oftentimes reclaims a vicious animal. A mean horse is apt to retaliate upon one who abuses him.

Before entering a horse's stall and when coming up behind him speak to him gently and approach him quietly. This will save you from being kicked. NEVER KICK A HORSE, STRIKE HIM ABOUT THE HEAD, OR BEAT HIM WITH A STICK OR CLUB. A horse should be punished only at the time when he commits an offense, and never while you are in anger.

Always give the horse an opportunity to drink before leaving the stables and putting the bit in the mouth. In cold weather you should warm the bit. Never take a rapid gait until the horse has been warmed up. A horse should be walked several hundred yards before starting on a trot. When a horse is brought in at night in a heated condition, never let him stand in a draft; always blanket him and rub down his legs, then walk him about until he cools off, and finish caring for him by turning up the hair with a brush until he is dry.

Never feed grain or fresh grass to a horse when he is heated; hay will not hurt him, no matter how warm he is. Never water a horse when he is heated unless you are to continue the patrol immediately. Sponging out the mouth and nostrils is very refreshing. Never throw water on any part of the horse when he is heated. Never allow a horse's back to be cooled suddenly. To cool the back gradually you should leave the saddle on for at least one-half hour after you dismount. Loosen your cinch. This will allow the flow of blood back into the veins gradually, and will often avoid a sore back. It is well to rub the back thoroughly after unsaddling. Never put a horse up for the night until he is thoroughly groomed. Be sure that his legs and pasterns are thoroughly cleaned.

Grooming

Grooming is essential to the general health and condition of the horse and is even more beneficial after a hard day's work, than in the morning. Horses improperly groomed, with ragged manes and long fetlocks, are indications of inefficient care. On the other hand, a well-groomed horse redounds to the credit of his rider and the organization to which he belongs.

To groom correctly, proceed as follows:

Take the currycomb in the right hand, fingers extended over the back of the comb, the brush in the left hand. First use currycomb on the near side of the horse, beginning at the neck just back of the ears, then chest, shoulders, near fore leg down to the knee, then back, flank, belly, loins and rump, then rear hind leg down to the hock. It is advisable to keep your left hand on the near side of the horse when using the currycomb or brush in case the horse should kick. This will automatically push you away and warn you the minute he is about to kick. To curry the off side of the horse, just change hands with brush and currycomb and proceed as before, striking the currycomb occasionally on the back of your brush to dislodge the dirt from it.

After you have proceeded to this point, lay down your currycomb, and brush all four legs, and pasterns, mane, forelock and tail. Don't be afraid to use your muscle in grooming a horse. A cloth may be used to finish the cleaning.

After wiping out nostrils and eyes, lift each foot and if it is not free from dirt, clean it with a hoof-pick, making sure that there is not a thing left in the hoof. Tails should be washed at least once a week, and the soft skin under the flank of the hind quarters should be kept soft and free from dirt. Clean the sheath once a month and your horse will be in a much healthier condition.

After a horse has traveled a long distance, hand-rubbing from the knee to the pastern is advised and very beneficial.

Watering

Never water a horse when he is warm. Water him before each meal. When traveling on the road water him frequently during the day. If he does not want water he will refuse it. A horse should have access to water at all times while in the stable. If it is impossible to water a horse before feeding, be sure that you wait two hours after he has been fed before you water him. In cold weather a horse does not require so much water, and watering three times a day is sufficient. In hot weather a horse requires from eight to fifteen gallons daily, of course depending on the temperature. When watering a horse in a stream remove the bit, if possible; if not, water him in deep water so that he may get his mouth in as far as necessary. Always water him facing down stream. This will prevent the water from rushing up his nose, which hinders him from obtaining a sufficient amount.

Feeding

A horse should be fed three times a day, morning, noon, and night. Four quarts of grain is approximately the correct amount for each feeding. Some horses thrive on more, some on less. Hay should be given once a day, usually at night, and about twelve to fifteen pounds. When feeding at night it is advised that you see to it that the horse eats a portion of his hay first before giving him his oats. He will get more benefit from them. The use of bran once or twice a week is very beneficial to the horse and whenever obtainable on the road you should give it. Salt should be occasionally given. Feeding of grass in the morning when the dew is on it acts as a tonic for the horse, and we advocate this.

If a horse should become sick or injured, it is advisable to discontinue feeding or at least reduce his ration.

Sick Horses

If you are unable to determine what the sickness is you should call the nearest veterinary, and then notify your commanding officer immediately.

Shoeing

A mounted policeman should familiarize himself with the correct manner of shoeing. Improper shoeing is the cause of a great deal of lameness. Shoes should be reset, or, if necessary, new ones put on, at least once a month.

All horses are not shod alike, therefore you should watch the shoeing when your horse is in the shop, for the rider knows better than the blacksmith what his horse should have.

Never ride a horse on hard pavements unless absolutely necessary, but keep on the shoulders of the highway.

Use a flat shoe in summer and calks in the winter, when conditions necessitate their use. If you are in a locality for the winter where they have deep snow, it is better to be without shoes.

Oiling the hoof occasionally is beneficial to the condition of the horse.

Riding

Never Lounge in the Saddle. If you do, this presses the bars on the rear of the saddle into the horse's back, and causes saddle sores, which are hard to heal, particularly when you have to continue patrolling. Your weight should be evenly distributed. You can easily do this by having the correct stirrup length. See that the two stirrups are of the same length. This is important.

Never use your spurs unless it is necessary. Never jerk the horse's mouth. Gentle pressure will bring about better results. Your horse should be so educated that he will answer the reins immediately, and so trained that you can control him with one hand.

Do not cinch your horse too tightly. See that your bit fits the horse's mouth correctly. Saddle-blanket should be refolded once a month, and occasionally cleaned. Leather equipment should be cleaned thoroughly by using some good soap at least once a week.

Fitting the Saddle

General applications are as follows:

The withers must not be pinched or pressed upon. The central line of the back must have no pressure on it. The shoulder-blades must have full and unhampered movement. The loins must not carry any weight. The weight must be carried upon the ribs through the medium of the muscles covering them. The weight must be evenly distributed over a surface which extends from the play of the shoulders to the last true rib. The above applies to all types of saddles that may be used.

XIV

THE PREPARATION AND TRIAL OF CRIMINAL PROSECUTIONS IN COURTS OF SPECIAL SESSIONS, POLICE COURTS AND JUSTICES' COURTS

The trial of any kind of proceeding before a law court consists in presenting what is called "evidence" to the consideration of the court in order to prove or disprove some matter or thing which is in dispute.

The means used to present the evidence is the testimony of witnesses—whether that testimony be given by word of mouth or by submitting documents or other things to the consideration of the court.

Centuries of experience have taught mankind that it is unsafe to rely upon the impressions that passing events make upon the human mind. One individual sees a thing happen or hears a conversation, and at once receives an impression from the occurrence or from the words utterly or slightly different from the impression produced on the mind of another person who sees the same thing or hears the same words.

Since abstract justice between human beings has always been and always will be the chief object of civilization and society, certain rules and regulations have been made and enforced in our law courts (which we call the law of evidence) which rules are made and enforced to guard against this well-known and inevitable charactertistic of human observation. A person is permitted to tell only what that person saw, or heard, or tasted, or felt, or smelled, and is not allowed to state *deductions* made from the use of the senses.

Since policemen are usually called upon to present the first obtainable evidences of crime, it is quite necessary they should have some idea of what evidence is and how to present it to the courts wherein they usually function as prosecuting officers or witnesses or both.

In the first place, then, bearing in mind the fact that society, represented by the court, is not interested in what you think, but only in what you know, it is a pretty safe rule when you are acting as a witness and giving testimony to say only such words as will describe what you have seen with your eyes, or heard with your ears, or smelled with your nose, or touched with your hands, or tasted with your tongue. In other words, the most direct evidence you can give is the impression you receive of an event through the medium of your five senses—namely, seeing, hearing, smelling, touching and tasting.

It may seem to be an easy matter to do this, but it isn't. Poets and philosophers, playwrights and actors, preachers and lawyers, doctors and scientists—in fact, every human being since articulate speech was first used by man has striven to express the sensations derived from the senses in simple words, and not one has ever completely succeeded.

So it is no wonder that when a policeman goes on the witness-stand to give his version of an event, which is very often the only evidence of a crime then available, he is constantly interrupted by objections and continuously assailed by innuendo and direct accusation of perjury by a highly trained and ofttimes highly paid specialist (whom we call a lawyer) whose life is spent in considering the various uses and abuses of words to convey the ideas and the workings of the human mind.

But, if policemen will remember the cardinal rule—namely, that the court (which term as I use it includes a jury, when there is one) is not concerned with what they *think* but only with what they *know,* and use their words accordingly—they can well afford to let the lawyers rage and imagine vain things; for when you talk about what you know from the use of your own senses you are pretty apt to talk convincingly.

And I might caution you, in this connection, never under any circumstances argue with the judge or with the lawyers when you are acting in the capacity of a witness.

As a witness you are at a disadvantage because you are not personally interested in the matter under investigation and can tell only what you know; and while your self-esteem and pride will suffer some terrible jolts, console yourself with the thought that the policeman, being a public servant, is, by the rules of the game of public life, a fair target for criticism and vilification and abuse. If you can not keep your temper under any and all conditions you had better follow some other profession such as bricklaying or even the practise of law, where you can speak your mind and relieve your feelings without damage to your employers —which in your case is Society, spelled with a capital S.

This elemental and elementary rule of evidence I have tried to formulate will stand you in good stead in preparing complaints and informations.

State the facts—state only the facts as you can prove them by your own testimony or the testimony of some other person, and you will seldom have your informations or complaints dismissed under any of the innumerable rules of pleading an adroit and skilful lawyer can always quote in the interests of his client.

"Make 'em short and make 'em snappy!" is a pretty good rule to follow when giving orders or laying an information.

Follow the same basic general principle when you are preparing a case for presentation wherein you must depend upon the information of some other person or persons to prove a crime has been committed. Don't let informants get you all steamed up by telling you what they think, or what they imagine, or what somebody else told them.

What somebody else said is hearsay evidence, and is not available for any purpose so far as a criminal investigation is concerned—except in the case of admissions or confessions by the accused.

What the witness thinks is of no consequence whatever—what you must be able to do is to show the court what he *knows,* and that he acquired that knowledge by the use of one of his five senses.

When you are called in to help a citizen in redressing a wrong he has suffered (or thinks he has), or when a citizen calls on you to make an arrest or to exercise any other authority you may have, the first thing for you to do is to get the facts, and that is a job lawyers find the most difficult of any they are called upon to do.

People are prone to touch but lightly on actions which reflect blame or censure on themselves and to magnify those acts and circumstances which have caused them annoyance, or damage, or harm.

You men are filling a long-felt want throughout this State and are called upon to add to the usual functions of a policeman some of those duties usually performed by a lawyer or a judge.

Cities and villages maintain their own municipal police forces whose duties are similar to yours, but you have the additional duty of preparing and presenting your cases to magistrates almost always unused to the forms and proceedings in a criminal action, and you must do this in the majority of your cases without help or assistance from any one.

Always remember that the burden is on you to present the facts which to your mind constitute a crime in an orderly, clear and coherent manner, avoiding the use of expressions such as "I think," "It seemed to me," or "It looked as tho," or similar expressions.

It is your duty to know, not to think.

It is your duty to comprehend completely any given situation before you act; when a thing only "seems" to be true, you assume a heavy responsibility if you act.

Moreover, in presenting a set of facts in such a way that your presentation does not carry conviction to the average mind you weaken your authority and the prestige of your corps.

I've forgotten who said, "Be sure you are right and then go ahead," but it's a mighty good rule to apply in a lawsuit or a criminal prosecution.

The great difficulty from the policeman's point of view is in knowing when you are right; but that's the whole trouble with any lawsuit.

Proper investigation with an eye only for facts and a complete disregard for inference or conclusion; a fair knowledge of the English language to enable you to express the knowledge you have acquired during that investigation, and an orderly habit of thought and expression so that you will be able to develop your story whether by your own testimony or that of some one else in such a way that the court will see the picture of the event just as you saw it, will enable you to perform your full duty as a peace officer of the state and will bring success to you in your work as a policeman.

When you go in to try a case before a justice of the peace, or to present the evidence you have obtained which to your mind indicates that a crime has been committed, and that there is reasonable grounds to believe that the accused person committed it, go over your own story in your mind and make sure you are going to tell only what you know, not what some one else told you.

When what some one else told you is a necessary part of the evidence which will prove the commission of the crime, go over that person's story with him or them as the case may be so as to be sure they are telling only what they know.

Then when you have the witnesses on the stand let them tell their story their own way.

The usual questions to arrive at this point are something like this:

"What is your name?

"Where do you live?

"Do you know the accused?

"Do you know anything about this case (or about the crime of which this defendant stands accused)?

"Now go ahead and tell the court in your own way just what you know."

In almost every case a witness will leave out of his testimony some statement you consider to be an important element in his story.

It is a good rule to allow the witness to finish his story in his own way and then to ask him questions which will enable him to supply in his own words the missing parts of his story that you think are important.

In many cases the judge won't allow you to do this.

In many other cases the defendant or his attorney

will object vociferously and insistently to your "leading" the witness or coaching him on the witness-stand.

Again let me remind you to keep your temper. Do not allow your attention to be distracted from the main point—which is to get *all* your witness' story before the court.

Each case must be handled differently and according to the peculiar conditions surrounding it. No hard and fast rule can be formulated. You must use your brains and your wits in protecting the public from criminals in such circumstances, just as you use your bodies and your courage in protecting it in other and different cases.

Having "put in your case," that is, having related to the court all you know, and having seen to it that your witnesses have done the same thing, you and your witnesses will be called upon to face a cross-examination.

Cross-examination is permitted only for the purpose of testing the truth of the story told to the court.

If you and your witnesses have told the truth; if you have followed the simple cardinal rule of making only those statements which will express in simple words the impression your five senses have conveyed to your brain concerning the events you are describing you need have no fear of being involved in any contradictions or mistakes.

Cross-examination is too often used for the purpose of browbeating or bullying witnesses even by the most distinguished and ethical members of the legal profession.

And here again let me caution you to hold your temper well in control; don't argue with the cross-examiner, and above all things don't give him any more information than he asks for; be courteous; be cool and be positive and certain in the use of the words you use to answer his questions.

The cross-examiner will undoubtedly attempt to compel you to answer "Yes" or "No" to his questions in order to so frame his question as to put you in a hole should you answer it that way.

The old story of the cross-examiner who having secured the consent of the witness to answer his questions "Yes" or "No," immediately asked him, "Have you quit beating your wife yet?" is quite in point. Don't get yourself, nor permit your witnesses to be put in that position.

Say you can't answer all questions "Yes" or "No," and if you are pressed too far go right to bat and say you *won't* be so bound.

If the judge directs you to answer "Yes" or "No," and you feel you can not do it, say so.

Of course, if the judge then directs you to answer that way, you must do it, but you will seldom meet with a judge willing to assume the responsibility of giving that direction, once you have said you can not so answer.

It's considered quite the thing in criminal cases— especially when the case is before a jury—to impute all kinds of cussedness and mischief and improper motives to policemen who are either appearing as witnesses or presenting the case.

As I told you a moment ago that is part of the game, and is an effort on the part of the defendant "to get your goat."

If you lose hold of that mythical animal, you are lost. For just as soon as a witness or a trial counsel—whether he be a layman or a lawyer—loses his temper, he loses his case.

Do not infer from what I have said that you are called upon to act as a persecutor instead of a prosecutor.

It is the duty of the district attorney to present such evidences of crime as you collect to the proper legal tribunal.

But you will be called upon in many cases to present the facts which led you to make an arrest, to a justice of the peace in some country town where they don't have a lawsuit oftener than once in four years and where the justices are usually business men or farmers who have but a slight idea of the extent of their authority and still less of an idea of how to exercise it.

It is to fit you to perform your duty on such an occasion that I am inflicting this lecture upon you in the hope that you will be able to give a good account of yourselves when called upon to present your case without expert aid or advice.

Remember, then, to be brief in your statements; use simple words and short sentences; speak in a clear, decided tone of voice and avoid oratory as you would the plague; don't argue with the judge, with opposing attorneys, or the witnesses; don't lose control of your temper or feelings and don't be astonished when about seventy per cent of your cases are thrown out of court.

XV

EXTRADITION AND RENDITION

It is asserted that the territorial limitation of continued political and military dominance before steam and motor transport was only the distance a horse could travel in a day from the conqueror's capital or base. The consequences of the development of transportation are likewise strikingly evident in the work of a police department conducting a border patrol as part of its routine in the rural districts. Access to New York from Canada and adjoining states by fugitives from justice is simple, and modern conceptions in administrative law disdain the ancient spirit, where when the hue and cry had pursued a sturdy rascal to the limits of a shire, the constables sat down quite satisfied they had well disposed of a most troublesome matter. Extradition, or more properly interstate rendition of criminals, therefore, has assumed an aspect of routine for the New York State Police.

The grades of the department active in the field are chiefly interested in the law governing their immediate actions where fugitives come into New York, rather than in the operation of the somewhat complicated legal machinery where it is necessary to return to this State one who has fled to another state or country. Suffice

it to say upon this subsidiary feature of the practise,
that where a wrongdoer flees to another state, it is usual
for the district attorney of the county where the crime
was committed to handle the request that our Governor
make requisition of the Governor of the asylum state;
where the criminal flees to a foreign country the same
official will supervise the application through the Governor and the Secretary of State of the United States

Peace officers of New York, for most practical purposes, have only to know that where a criminal eludes
them here and flees to another jurisdiction that the law
of New York empowering the officer ends at the bound-
ary of the State. Outside our jurisdiction, a New
York policeman has not even the authority of a citizen
of the asylum state to apprehend a culprit, unless our
officers may by courtesy be armed with the warrant of
the Governor whose sanction permits the enforced return of the culprit here. Where a criminal flees from
New York it is, therefore, generally best that the policeman consult with his superiors, or with the district
attorney. However, the cases in which criminals come
into the State require more detailed comment.

It is no longer open to question that where there are
reasonable grounds to believe that a felony has been
committed in another jurisdiction by a person who has
come into this State, a peace officer may make an arrest
without a warrant as tho the felony had been committed here. The grounds of belief may come through
reliable communications from police officers in the state
whence the criminal fled, or other information upon

which a reasonable man should rely. Authentic tele-
grams and telephone messages have been held sufficient
in cases of emergency to fortify the act of the arresting
officer before the Governor acts or consents to act. This
is a rule of necessity, for surely it is seldom possible to
await the tedious process of demand and rendition, later
described, before arresting a criminal on the alert and
ready to flee elsewhere. Yet the policeman receiving
news of the presence of a criminal in this State may
protect himself, where time and circumstances do not
press, by judicial process through a warrant obtained
from any magistrate. This may be done while the
requisition is awaited from the state or territory whence
the criminal fled. The prisoner whether arrested
under a warrant or without must be brought before the
magistrate and the proceedings are the same as in an
ordinary case. However, instead of word-of-mouth evidence as to the prisoner's guilt, an exemplified copy
of any indictment found against him in a demanding
state may be offered in evidence of the charge. The
magistrate then may commit the accused until rendition
papers can be made out. A time is specified in the commitment, and if the demanding state does not proceed
within that time, the prisoner is released. He may also
be admitted to bail, and the district attorney notifies
the executive authority of the state whence he fled.

Now begins the true process of interstate rendition.
The Governor of the state whence the criminal fled
makes demand upon the Governor of New York. The
practise in the Executive Chamber is to require a certifi-

cate from the Governor of the demanding state with a warrant, complaint, indictment or affidavit setting forth that a crime has been committed. The offense charged may not be recognized as a crime at all in New York, and it may be only a misdemeanor. The certificate must further show that the accused was in the demanding state at the time of the crime and that the accused has fled therefrom to escape responsibility. Further, the certificate affirmatively shows that the demand for rendition is not for the purpose of merely collecting a civil debt, but is for the purpose of criminal prosecution in good faith. When the Governor of New York is satisfied with the proof so submitted he issues his extradition warrant. The fugitive is then sought with this or if he has previously been arrested under a magistrate's warrant or has been committed by a magistrate after arrest without a warrant, the Governor's warrant is served upon the prisoner. The extradition warrant is good in the hands of the representative of the demanding state to take the accused back for trial. Under the laws of the United States the officer may pass through several states on his way home and the New York warrant is good even in such states to protect the officer in the possession of his prisoner.

Before this is done the accused may demand a hearing before the Governor upon the ground that he is not the same person named in the certificate of the demanding state, or that he was not in the state at the time of the crime or that there is no prosecution in good faith pending and that his rendition is sought for ulterior improper purposes and upon various other grounds. Before the Governor will issue his warrant he will hear what the accused has to say and in some cases withhold his warrant. Then the demanding state is without remedy to review the action of the Governor. Later the Governor may still reopen the matter if further evidence is submitted to him. Likewise the Governor may issue several warrants if the first is lost or is irregular or is not served.

The accused also may ask for a writ of habeas corpus in the courts of New York and in the federal courts. Many of the questions threshed out before the Governor may be gone over again there. In some cases an accused when captured may even consent to go back to the state with the officers where the crime occurred and not insist that he be extradited. When once he is back where he belongs the trial courts seldom examine too closely how he got there; but the Governor of the asylum state has in some cases sued out a writ of habeas corpus in the federal courts where it was claimed the accused was kidnaped from the asylum state.

There is an elaborate set of rules drawn up by the Governor's office for those cases in which a criminal has fled from New York State. As has been said, the application is made upon the Governor by the district attorney of the county where the crime occurred for requisition to the asylum state. The purpose of these rules in the main insures that the demand is made in good faith and that one really guilty of a crime shall be prosecuted by public officials. Every circumstance must be explained that would cast any doubt upon this.

Interstate rendition has its origin in article 4, section 2, of the United States Constitution requiring that fugitives from justice be given up on demand by the state to which they flee. International or foreign extradition is sanctioned by international law, but particularly by the treaties the United States may have with foreign governments. It is useless here to digest these treaty provisions. Most countries, however, have agreed with us to render up those accused of the more serious crimes. Upon proper instructions it may be necessary for state policemen to arrest under the same circumstances as fugitives from other states persons who flee from foreign countries. Ordinarily the request for an arrest may come through the Governor of New York. There may be cases in which the request may come directly to the police and then they should exercise the same discretion. The demand for criminals escaping from New York to a foreign country are ordinarily conveyed to the State Department at Washington through Executive Chamber channels.

In completion of this outline, it should be noted that in New York we have a law relative to the rendering up of witnesses. Oftentimes it is difficult to prosecute because an important witness would leave the state and thus defy the subpena-servers. The states bordering on New York have agreed with New York to render up witnesses needed in criminal trials in the several states. This is done by court order, and the statute authorizing it in New York has been held constitutional in the state courts.

Our country doubtless will continue to approach complete unity, and state lines will decrease in significance. The subject of interstate rendition therefore warrants study by state troopers as one likely to grow in daily usefulness.

PART II

I

CRIME AND CRIME CLASSIFICATION

The policeman's study is a study of law and statutes, especially the criminal and penal violations, for he is an executive officer of government charged with the enforcement of the laws.

Our government is divided into three branches, each having its particular function to perform and its separate work to do. The legislative branch declares what the law shall be and accordingly adopts such measures as are necessary for the conduct and regulation of society in general. The second branch, known as the executive, then functions to enforce such laws and to this branch belong the police. In order to secure proper interpretation of the laws it was necessary to create the judicial branch, whose duty is defined not only to interpret the laws but to punish violators of them.

The function of one branch can not be performed by another; the police can not make laws nor can they punish offenders. They must enforce the law as made by the legislature and where a violation occurs, bring the offender before the judicial branch for trial and adjudication of the offense.

A crime is any act or omission forbidden by law and punishable upon conviction by penal discipline. No crime occurs, therefore, unless there is a law forbidding the act or the omission in question, and even tho a policeman may consider the doing of an act as against public policy such act is not a crime unless it is expressly forbidden by legislative enactment. The executive officer accepts that which is ordained as law by the legislature and enforces those provisions only, without regard to what his opinion may be as to what should be law.

In further analyzing the definition of crime we find that a crime may be committed not only by an act performed but by an omission to act when an act is required. A person who shoots and kills another through the act of shooting commits homicide, but where the statutes provide that a person causing an automobile accident is charged to report such accident to the proper authorities, his failure to so report is a crime because he has omitted to perform an act which by law he is commanded to perform.

Crimes are divided into two general classes, felonies and misdemeanors, and it is most necessary that the policeman be familiar with the grade of crime at hand, for in felonies he is granted wider powers of arrest than in misdemeanors. A felony comprises the more serious division and is a crime which is or may be punishable by death or imprisonment in a state prison. In our state the law provides that no person shall be sentenced to a state prison for a less term than one year so that the punishment prescribed for the offense at hand will usually determine its grade.

Misdemeanors, the lower grade of crimes, usually carry a penalty of less than one year and sentence upon conviction is to a county jail or penitentiary. There are a few exceptions to this general rule, however, for we have a few crimes, specified as misdemeanors, which carry a greater penalty. These are so few in number that we will not take them up at this time.

The parties to a crime are either principals or accessories. A principal is a person concerned in the commission of a crime, whether he directly commits the act constituting the offense or aids and abets in its commission, and whether present or absent; and a person who directly or indirectly counsels, commands, induces, or procures another to commit a crime.

A person residing in some distant state might be a principal to a homicide committed in this state altho such person was many miles from the scene of the crime at the time it was committed provided he in any way advised the commission of the crime and was responsible through inducement or procurement in having some other person perform the act. Likewise, one who watches outside a house while a confederate burglarizes the premises, the purpose of the watcher being to give alarm in case of approach of any person, is a principal to the crime of burglary.

An accessory is a person *who, after the commission of a felony,* harbors, conceals, or aids the offender, with intent that he may avoid or escape from arrest, trial, conviction or punishment, having knowledge or reasonable grounds to believe that such offender is liable to arrest, has been arrested, is indicted or convicted, or has committed a *felony*.

From the above, you will note that accessories are concerned only in felony cases and a person performing such acts after a misdemeanor (which would make him an accessory if the crime were a felony), would be a principal to the misdemeanor. In other words, there are no accessories in misdemeanor cases, all concerned being principals.

There is also what is known as an attempt to commit a crime, which is any act done with intent to commit the crime and tending, but failing, to effect its commission. An arrest may be made for an attempt to commit a crime and a person may be convicted for the attempt. The punishment for the attempt, however, is not as great as if the offense were actually consummated.

There are certain classes of persons deemed incapable of committing crime. The first of these is a child under the age of seven and the statutes provide that irrespective of what acts he may do such child can not be charged with crime. Likewise, between the ages of seven and twelve there is a presumption of law whereby such children can not know the difference between right and wrong, and consequently are incapable of committing crime. However, this presumption may be removed by the prosecution provided it can show that such child has sufficient mental development to know the nature of the act. It is a rather difficult problem, however, to remove such presumption, but this is work for the prosecuting officers rather than for the police. It is very advisable never to arrest any child under the age of twelve for a criminal offense.

A child between the ages of twelve and sixteen, committing an offense which if committed by an adult would be a crime, is not charged with the crime itself but with juvenile delinquency. This section applies in all cases except those which may be punishable by death or life imprisonment and in these instances you should consult with the district attorney before taking action in making the complaint.

Insane persons, so adjudged by competent authority, are likewise considered irresponsible for their actions and incapable therefore of a criminal intent, as are persons who commit crime while in a state of involuntary intoxication. For your purposes, however, in law enforcement you may disregard all other provisions of capacity except those applying to children.

The study of crimes covers a very large field, as each particular crime necessitates the presence of certain elements and in the loss of one of those elements the offense is changed to some other crime. The general scope of the policeman's work has been very ably summed up into five fundamental principles and a case proper for police action should be classified under one of these:

1. To preserve the peace.
2. To enforce the laws.
3. To prevent and detect crime.

4. To protect life and property.

5. To arrest violators of the law.

In your daily activities analyze each act you perform so that you may be readily able to classify under just which principle you are operating. A matter which can not be included under one of the five is not a proper matter for police attention.

Again, as a groundwork for the study of crime investigation, fix firmly in your mind the three important things to do upon reaching the scene of a crime and never fail to apply them at the proper time. Of course the most essential thing is the arrest of the perpetrator of such crime, but this is not always possible, for in most instances you will find that he has fled or is not in the immediate vicinity.

It is then important that you begin to gather the names and addresses of your witnesses and get such information as they possess relative to the offense.

The next thing to do is to safeguard all evidence for future use. This means to take possession of it and to properly mark it for future identification.

Many times failures of the investigating officer to comply with the last two duties has resulted in loss of the case and in eagerness to arrest the offender all else has been lost sight of. An arrest without witnesses and evidence will be of very little value.

Resolve that when you bring in a case to a prosecuting officer it will be complete in every detail, at least as far as you are able to complete it, for you are at the scene of the crime and possibly are the only person in a real position to know just what took place and what will be necessary to tell and show to the court at the trial.

A policeman must constantly study the penal provisions of our laws in order to keep up with the amendments thereto. No police officer should be without a good edition of the penal law and every spare moment should be given to its study. You must carry your knowledge in your head, for at a moment when you are called upon to act there is very little time for reference to a book. Be sure of yourself at all times. Never assume what the law is, but rather know just what the statute provides on the case at hand. An error in behalf of an offender is more easily corrected than one from overzealousness or ignorance on the part of the officer.

The statutes provide, usually, the grade of crime and the punishment for the act or omission specified. However, in some cases an act or omission is forbidden and there is no specification as to the degree of crime or the punishment. It is provided that where the performance of an act is prohibited by statute and no penalty for violation of such statute is imposed in any statute, the doing of such act is a misdemeanor. A person convicted of any crime declared to be a misdemeanor and for which no punishment is especially prescribed by any statute, may be punishable by imprisonment in a county jail or penitentiary for not more than one year or by a fine of not more than five hundred dollars, or both.

Where any statute makes a crime punishable by a fine and the amount of the fine is not specified, a fine of not more than five hundred dollars may be imposed. A person convicted of a crime declared to be a felony, and for which no punishment is specially prescribed by any statute, is punishable by imprisonment for not more than seven years, or by a fine of not more than one thousand dollars, or both. In all cases where a corporation is convicted of an offense, for the commission of which a natural person would be convicted of a felony, such corporation is punishable by a fine of not more than five thousand dollars.

II

ARREST

Of the duties delegated to the policeman perhaps there is none he will be called upon to exercise more often than that of arrest, and it should be done with care and strictly within the provisions of the statutes on the subject. Volumes have been written and many court decisions rendered concerning arrests, so that it would not be possible to take this subject up in every detail. It must be borne in mind, however, that both the Constitutions of the State of New York and the United States provide that "no person shall be deprived of life, liberty or property without due process of law," and it behooves the officer charged with enforcing the law to understand thoroughly the limitations of his powers of arrest and to know that these powers are, in most instances, shared equally by the humblest person.

Arrest is the taking into custody of a person that he may be held to answer for a crime, and it is made by actual restraint of the person or by his voluntary submission to custody. Personal liberty has been construed to mean that one may change situation, move about as he may choose, or in fact do as he pleases so long as his movements and actions do not interfere with the property or rights of others or transgress upon the laws of the land.

Any one who infringes upon personal or property rights of others or transgresses upon the laws of the land should forfeit this personal liberty by detention to answer for the crime.

It is very important, however, to note that the fact of the arresting restraint is not in itself an absolute indication that the person arrested is guilty of the crime for which he is being detained. His detention is merely for the purpose of holding him to answer before a judicial tribunal for the adjudication of the offense to be proved in the manner prescribed by statute.

Before an arrest will be justified there must be a crime for which it is probable that the arrested party may be convicted, or in other words there must be an actual violation of law. Nothing is law unless it is so ordained to be by the highest power in the state created with legislative or lawmaking functions, and therefore no act could be a violation of law merely because one's perception indicates that it should be. The statutes define the law, and a violation of such statutes is a crime—nothing else.

If there has been no crime there can be no arrest. Mere suspicion that a crime has been committed will not justify an arrest. You may suspect the person of the crime, but never are you permitted to suspect the crime. That must occur in actuality.

Unlawful and malicious arrests not only violate the constitutional rights of the detained person, but render the officer concerned liable for damages and punishment. Harsh measures and undue severity can not be resorted to, for it is plainly provided that only such force as is absolutely necessary to take or retain a person in your custody is permissible; superfluous force renders the officer liable for assault both civilly and criminally. The grade of the crime is likewise a very determining factor as to what amount of force may be used. In misdemeanor cases very little physical power is permitted to be exercised in accomplishing an arrest, while it has been held that in felony cases the taking of human life would be justified by the arresting officer should all other means of capture or retention fail.

Sound judgment coupled with extreme care is necessary when resorting to force as an adjunct to arrest. Very often the overbearing attitude and discourteous treatment of the defendant by an officer will result in resistance, whereas a good level-headed policeman seldom, if ever, finds difficulty in executing this function.

Arrests are made by peace officers armed with warrants, by peace officers without warrants and by private persons. Peace officers are sheriffs, their under-sheriffs and deputies, detectives, constables, marshals, police constables, policemen in cities, towns and villages, and state troopers. There are also other classes of peace officers created for special purposes such as game wardens, railroad and steamboat police, etc., but these are usually ordained with the powers of peace officers for the purpose of enforcing the particular laws under which they were created. Our study will now be based on the arrests made by peace officers armed with a warrant of arrest.

A warrant of arrest is an order in writing issued by a magistrate directed generally to a peace officer commanding him to arrest the person or persons named within the warrant, and bring such person or persons before the issuing magistrate or before some other magistrate designated in the warrant, or in case there is no magistrate designated other than the issuing magistrate and he is not available, before the nearest and most accessible magistrate having jurisdiction to hear the charge.

Under this method of arrest the officer is acting with judicial sanction and upon receiving a warrant he should examine it to see that it is sufficiently clear as to the crime charged and the persons named therein for apprehension. In other words, arrests on warrants should be made only when the warrant itself is valid and issued by a magistrate having jurisdiction to issue a warrant for the offense named therein.

The validity of the warrant should again be examined as to time for service. If the crime charged therein be a *misdemeanor,* such warrant may be executed only in the *day time* of a business day and *not on Sunday.* Generally each form of warrant bears a printed space for the magistrate's endorsement rendering the warrant valid at any time of the day, night or Sunday, and it is recommended in accepting a warrant for service that the officer, upon noting that the warrant charges a *misdemeanor,* request that the magistrate place his endorsement thereon so that the difficulty of arresting on Sunday or at night may be overcome. *Felony* warrants *are good for service at any time of the day, night or Sunday* without the foregoing endorsement. This is of utmost importance.

There is a further limitation placed on warrants of arrest as to the place of service, and this provision is a very important one from the policeman's point of view. In your future study of magistrates and courts you will find a division between the higher and lower ones as to jurisdiction and powers. Generally the lower courts are spoken of as courts of Special Sessions and are presided over by justices of the peace, police magistrates, and police judges in cities, town and villages. The higher courts with which a police officer will have to deal are the County Courts and the Supreme Courts. A warrant of arrest issued by a justice of the peace, police magistrate, or police judge is usually good within the county where it was issued only, and if the party to be apprehended by virtue of such warrant is in another county the warrant must be presented by the officer to a magistrate within the county wherein the arrest is to be made for his endorsement, or in other words for his permission to serve such warrant within such county.

In the creation of police courts in some cities it is especially provided by charter that the Special Sessions judges in that city may issue warrants of arrest which are good for service in any part of the state without endorsement, but as a general rule a warrant from a Special Sessions court is good only within the county wherein it was issued unless endorsed as above explained.

On the other hand a warrant from a magistrate of a County or Supreme Court is good anywhere within the State without endorsement.

A very important provision is that governing arrests in counties other than a county wherein the warrant in question was issued. We will assume for example that you are a peace officer in Albany County and while in that county you are given a warrant, charging a *misdemeanor,* for the arrest of a person who you learn is in the County of Oneida. This warrant has been issued by a justice of the peace and on the face of it service would be valid in Albany County only. You journey to Oneida County and go before any magistrate of that county and request that he endorse such warrant that you may serve it within Oneida County.

The form for endorsement is printed on most forms of warrants and after you fill out your part, wherein you swear that you are familiar with the handwriting of the issuing magistrate and that the signature thereon is genuine, the Oneida County magistrate affixes his endorsement permitting you to make the arrest in Oneida County.

From the above you will learn that the officer having a warrant endorsed must be familiar with the handwriting of the issuing magistrate, otherwise he can not swear that the signature is genuine. After the endorsement has been secured you apprehend the person named within the warrant. If the above warrant charged a felony the procedure would be the same. It is a matter of the jurisdiction of the magistrate rather than the grade of the crime which makes endorsements for service in other counties necessary.

Again, assume that in the above arrest for a misdemeanor the person apprehended declines to return to Albany County immediately. It is such person's privilege upon demand, after having been arrested for a misdemeanor, to be taken before a magistrate in the county of arrest for admission to bail that he may appear at a later date in the County of Albany to answer the charge. Upon such demand the officer must comply by taking him to a magistrate for bail. The bail so taken is then conveyed from Oneida County to the issuing magistrate in Albany County by the arresting officer. This provision does not apply to arrests for felonies, for in these cases the prisoner must be taken back immediately to the issuing magistrate or to some other magistrate in the county wherein the offense was committed.

In making service under a warrant the following steps should be observed by the officer to insure proper service:

1. Announce your authority by stating your name, department and rank.

2. Ascertain from the party you are about to arrest if he is the party named in such warrant.

3. Inform the party of the charge for which he is being arrested.

4. Permit him to see the warrant should he so demand, being careful that such warrant is not destroyed or mutilated by him.

The arrest is then accomplished by restraining such person or by his voluntary submission to custody, and the prisoner is then conveyed without undue delay before a magistrate.

After bringing a prisoner into court the officer then makes what is called his return to the warrant; that is, he fills in on the proper space of the warrant his specification that the command of the warrant has been complied with and that the prisoner is now before the court. The arraignment of the prisoner then proceeds and the manner in which this is done will be explained in a later lecture.

The coroner of a county may issue a warrant of arrest for the apprehension of a person responsible for the death of a human being, and such warrant may be executed in any part of the State without endorsement.

There are also warrants of arrest known as bench-warrants which derive their name from the fact that they are issued from the bench by the court itself, and generally after an indictment has been found or in case of a contempt of court, or for the arrest of a person who has failed to obey a proper order of the court. These are served and executed in the same manner as any other warrant of arrest, but because they originate in a County or Supreme Court, they may be served in any part of the state without endorsement, which facilitates their execution.

Very often it occurs in criminal cases that a warrant is issued for a person whose true name is unknown, and a fictitious name is inserted in the body of the warrant, such as "John Doe, whose true name is unknown." Care must be exercised in executing such a warrant, for it designates a fictitious name with no positive means of identification, thus making it an easy matter for the officer to apprehend the wrong party. No arrests should be made under John Doe warrants unless the arresting officer is in possession of positive knowledge that the person he is about to apprehend is actually the person wanted for the offense.

To serve and execute a warrant of arrest an officer is justified in breaking into or out of any building, but before his breaking is permitted he must notify the occupants there of *his authority and purpose and demand admittance.* Such being refused he may then break any door or window to gain entrance, or if locked into a building he may break out.

Every person is bound to aid an officer in making an arrest or in retaining prisoners in his custody, and the refusal of any person so to aid after a proper demand by the officer is a misdemeanor on the part of such person.

Warrants of arrest issued within this state are good for service within the boundaries of this state only and should the person to be apprehended flee into some other state it is necessary to resort to rendition or extradition proceeding for his return. This subject is treated later in the course.

One warrant of arrest may direct the apprehension of any number of persons as named within the warrant.

Arrest By a Peace Officer Without a Warrant

The number of arrests you will make without warrants will greatly exceed those wherein you receive that judicial sanction. The criminal code especially states when this power may be exercised and we will take up each instance for discussion, so that there may be no chance for mistake.

First. You are permitted to arrest without a warrant for any crime, either felony or misdemeanor, committed or attempted in your presence. The crime must actually be committed or some act extended toward its commission, and no arrest is justified wherein there is merely a suspicion that a crime has been committed or attempted.

Second. You may arrest without a warrant when the person has committed a felony, altho such felony was not committed in your presence. To justify an arrest under this section you must have positive knowledge of two things: first that felony was committed and second that the person you are about to arrest committed the felony. As an instance of an arrest by this authority we will assume that you have knowledge through a published circular that a grand larceny has been committed and on such circular is a photograph of the person committing such crime. This larceny may have been committed at some distant point, but through the medium of the circular you know that it has been committed and through the photograph of the accused you know when you meet him that he is actually the person who committed the felony altho it was not committed in your presence. By authority of this section you are permitted to make the arrest.

Third. You may arrest without a warrant when a felony has in fact been committed and you have reasonable grounds to believe that the person you are about to arrest committed such felony. This is commonly called an arrest on suspicion and in such cases again you will note that the crime can not be suspected. There must have been a felony in fact committed and you must have reasonable grounds for your suspicions. We will assume that you are notified by telephone that a certain dwelling-house has just been entered by a thief and a large quantity of silverware has been taken. A short time later you discover a man in the act of selling some silverware and upon your questioning of him he can not give a reasonable explanation as to how he came into possession of such articles. You would then be justified in detaining him, for you have knowledge that a felony has been committed and can show a reasonable belief that this person may have been the thief. The law shields the police officer in arrests of this nature provided he can show reasonable cause for the arrest. If no felony has in fact been committed, then such an arrest without a warrant is unlawful may be resisted.

In the study of the above you will see that an ar. for a misdemeanor is justified without a warrant only when the offense is committed or attempted in the presence of the officer, while in felony cases the officer need not witness the crime committed so long as he knows the felony has been committed, and has either positive knowledge or reasonable suspicion that the person he is about to arrest committed such felony.

A peace officer may also, at night, without a warrant, arrest any person whom he has reasonable cause for believing has committed a felony, and is justified in making the arrest, tho it afterward appear that a felony had been committed, but that the person arrested did not commit it.

In making arrests without warrants you are permitted to use only such necessary force as will accomplish your purpose, as explained in a previous lecture, and you may break into or out of a building to effect an arrest just the same as if you were armed with a warrant.

Under act of Congress June 18, 1898, deserters from the army, navy, or marine corps may be arrested without warrants, and such deserters should be conducted to the nearest army post or naval station and turned over to the authorities at that place.

Any person apparently insane and conducting himself in a manner which in a sane person would be disorderly, may be arrested by any peace officer and confined in some safe and comfortable place until the question of his sanity be determined, as prescribed by the insanity laws. The officer making such arrest must immediately notify the health officer of the town, village, or city wherein the arrest of said person is made. The use of force or violence to take or retain such a person in custody is not unlawful provided only such force is used as is actually necessary to accomplish the purpose.

Private persons may arrest for a crime committed or attempted in their presence, also when a felony has been committed altho not in their presence, but they can not arrest on suspicion as a peace officer can. A private person making an arrest must take the prisoner without unnecessary delay before a magistrate, or turn the prisoner over to a peace officer for arraignment before a magistrate.

In many cases you will be called upon to arrest for a misdemeanor which you have not witnessed, and perhaps there may be reasons whereby it would defeat the ends of justice were you to delay the arrest until a warrant might be secured. In those cases you could have some person who witnessed the misdemeanor committed actually make the arrest and turn the prisoner over to you. In such a case be sure to have the person who makes the arrest accompany you to the court so that such person may make the charge against the prisoner.

Below are given a few decisions in connection with arrests:

Arrest at night on a warrant for a misdemeanor upon which a direction for such arrest is not endorsed by the magistrate is a false imprisonment.

An actual touching of the body is not required to constitute an arrest; it is sufficient if the party is within the power of the officer and submits to restraint.

If a felony has actually been committed, an officer, in arresting the offender or preventing his escape, will be justified in taking his life, provided there is an absolute necessity for doing so. It is otherwise in case of an arrest for a misdemeanor.

Except in the case of a felony, a peace officer can arrest without a warrant only for a crime committed or attempted in his presence.

III

MAGISTRATES AND COURTS

A person charged with a crime must be immediately brought before a magistrate after arrest. It is quite essential that the policeman be familiar with the procedure in courts, for there are times when he will be called upon to present the people's side of the case, or at least conduct matters until the arrival of the prosecuting officer. In all criminal actions, the matter is prosecuted in the name of the people of the State of New York against the offender, for a violation of the penal provisions of law is deemed a wrong against the people at large rather than a private offense, consequently it is prosecuted in their name. The arrested party is designated as the defendant and will be referred to hereafter as such.

Magistrates are public officers, having power to issue warrants for the arrest of persons charged with crimes, and are designated by statute in this State as follows:

> Justice of the Supreme Court
> Judges of any City Court
> County Judges and Special County Judges
> The City Judge of the City of New York and the
> Judges of the Court of General Sessions in the City and County of New York.

The Justices of the Peace.

The Police and other Special Justices appointed or elected in a City, Village, or Town.

The Mayors and Recorders of Cities.

The Judges of the City Court of Buffalo.

The Coroner of a County (for the purpose of issuing warrants of arrest for persons charged with the death of a human being through criminal means only).

Generally speaking, courts are divided into two classes, high and low. The lower ones are called courts of special sessions, usually presided over by justices of the peace, police judges, and police magistrates. These special sessions courts are inferior and their jurisdiction of offenses is limited to those specified in section 56 of the Code of Criminal Procedure, and only such crimes as are therein specified may be tried and determined before such a court. There are a few exceptions to this, for in the creation of special sessions courts in some cities a wider jurisdicton has been conferred by municipal regulation, governed by statute.

We will now take up step by step the procedure in a misdemeanor case before a special sessions court.

The arresting officer first determines by reference to section 56 the original jurisdiction of the offense, and the matter is then handled through the following channels:

1. Deposition of witness or witnesses to be alleged crime is taken, reduced to writing and sworn to before the magistrate. This deposition is simply a sworn

statement alleging facts which would indicate a crime.

2. An information is then drawn in legal form, signed and sworn to by the person informing or complaining of the crime before the magistrate. This is sometimes termed "laying an information," and correct forms for each particular crime will be found in the Code of Criminal Procedure.

3. A warrant of arrest is then issued by the magistrate. This is an order in writing directed generally to a peace officer, commanding that the person or persons named in such warrant be taken into custody and brought before the magistrate designated in such warrant.

4. The peace officer then makes the arrest and brings the defendant before the magistrate as directed.

5. When a defendant is returned to court, the peace officer executes a return to the warrant. This return is printed on most forms of warrants and is for the purpose of specifying that the command of the warrant has been complied with.

6. The prisoner is then arraigned on the charge; that is, the depositions and information are read to him by the magistrate and he is informed of his rights. It is most important that the greatest care be observed to see that these are fully and clearly stated to each defendant in a criminal action. Such rights are given below:

(a) To a speedy and public trial and to a trial by jury should the defendant so elect.

(b) To obtain counsel and to a reasonable time to procure counsel. The peace officer must without fee take a message to such counsel as designated by the defendant, should the defendant so demand.

(c) To secure witnesses in his behalf and to an adjournment for a reasonable time to secure such witnesses.

(d) To the right to confront witnesses against him, and to examine such witnesses, their depositions or informations either by himself or by his counsel.

(e) The right to bail during his adjournment. Bail is an absolute right in misdemeanor cases, and must be granted to a defendant at any time he so demands. In felony cases it is otherwise, and entirely at the discretion of the court.

(f) The right to have his case go before the grand jury rather than have it tried in special sessions court upon the execution of the certificate mentioned in section 57 Code of Criminal Procedure.

7. The defendant is then required to plead to the charge and such plea of guilty or not guilty is recorded by the magistrate.

8. Should the defendant plead guilty upon arraignment, and waive all rights, the magistrate then sentences him in accordance with the punishment prescribed for the offense.

9. Should the defendant plead not guilty and waive

his rights to a trial by jury, the magistrate proceeds to hear the evidence and testimony, and if the magistrate be convinced from such that the alleged crime was committed, and the defendant committed it, sentence is then imposed in accordance with the punishment prescribed. Should the magistrate be not convinced that the crime was committed, and that there was insufficient evidence to warrant conviction, the defendant must be discharged from custody forthwith.

10. Should the defendant plead not guilty upon arraignment, and demand a jury trial, the magistrate then complies with the provisions of section 703 of the Code of Criminal Procedure, and summons a panel of jurors to hear the case. The panel consists of twelve men, and from these twelve is selected a jury of six to try the issue. The evidence and testimony is then submitted to the jury and they retire and deliberate as to whether it is sufficient or not to convict. Their finding is called a verdict, and must be unanimous. If it be "guilty" the defendant is then sentenced by the magistrate, but if "not guilty" he must be immediately discharged from custody. It is a constitutional provision that no person may be placed in jeopardy twice for the same offense.

11. Should a defendant be convicted of a crime in special sessions court, he has the right of appeal to the county judge, but such appeal must be taken within sixty days after rendition of judgment.

12. Should the defendant be unable to furnish the required bail he may be committed to jail while await-

ing trial. Should a defendant be sentenced to jail, the peace officer conveying him there must deliver with the prisoner a commitment paper, authorizing the detention. This commitment is secured from the magistrate.

13. Should the peace officer make an arrest for a misdemeanor in some county other than the one wherein the warrant was issued, the defendant must, on demand, be taken before a magistrate in the county of arrest where he may give bail for his appearance at a later date in the county of the offense. This bail must be carried back to the issuing magistrate by the peace officer.

14. Should the arrest be made by an officer without a warrant, paragraphs 1, 2, 3, 4, and 5 are complied with after the prisoner is before the court. It has been held that where an arrest is made without a warrant, for an offense of which a justice of the peace has exclusive jurisdiction, no written information need be made or filed, nor warrant issued, where the defendant pleads guilty upon arraignment, and, further, that where a person is seized in the act of committing a crime and immediately taken before a court there is no necessity for a warrant. It is recommended, however, that all of the above steps be taken to insure a proper presentation of the case.

Your special attention is called to one provision of section 56 which is quoted herewith: "When a complaint is made to or a warrant issued by a committing magistrate for *any misdemeanor* not included in the foregoing subdivisions of this section, if the accused shall elect to be tried by a court of special sessions the Justice may proceed with the trial. But this subdivision shall not apply to any misdemeanor which is or may be punishable by a fine exceeding fifty dollars or by imprisonment exceeding six months."

Upon your reference therefore to section 56 should you not find the particular crime included therein, and it be one the maximum punishment for which is fifty dollars or six months, it may be tried in such court upon obtaining the consent of the defendant. This does not apply to any misdemeanor carrying a greater fine or longer imprisonment. These are called indictable misdemeanors and are handled through the same course as a felony.

IV

MAGISTRATES AND COURTS (*Continued*)

You have previously learned procedure in a special sessions court covering a misdemeanor case over which the court had exclusive jurisdiction, and we will now take up the course of an indictable misdemeanor and a felony case, the procedure in both being the same. In such cases the magistrate does not sit as a court, for he has no power to try and determine the offense. He simply sits as a committing magistrate for the purpose of determining whether there is probable cause to believe the crime was committed, and sufficient grounds to hold the accused for the action of a higher court through the process of indictment. Irrespective of the degree of the crime, the peace officer brings the defendant before a special sessions court, and if the crime be an indictable misdemeanor or a felony, the defendant is given an examination or hearing rather than a trial. The procedure is as follows:

1. Same as previous misdemeanor case.
2. Same as previous misdemeanor case.
3. Same as previous misdemeanor case.
4. Same as previous misdemeanor case.
5. Same as previous misdemeanor case.
6. The prisoner is then arraigned on the charge;

that is, the information and depositions are read to him by the magistrate. He is then informed of his rights, which are as follows:

(a) To an examination of the charge before such magistrate to determine if there be sufficient evidence to cause such magistrate· to hold the defendant for the action of the grand jury.

(b) To obtain counsel, and to a reasonable time to procure counsel.

(c) The right to secure witnesses and to an adjournment for a reasonable time to secure witnesses.

(d) The right to confront witnesses against him.

(e) The right to bail during the period of adjournment, in the discretion of the court.

(f) The right to waive the examination and have his case go before the grand jury.

7. The defendant is then required to plead either guilty or not guilty through the charge.

8. Should he plead guilty or not guilty and waive examination, the magistrate must hold him for the action of the grand jury. The committing magistrate may grant him bail provided the crime is not punishable by more than five years' imprisonment. Where the punishment is greater, bail can only be granted by a county judge or a justice of the supreme court. If the bail be not furnished, the prisoner must be committed to jail to await the action of the grand jury, and a commitment paper must accompany him.

9. Should the prisoner plead not guilty and demand

an examination the magistrate must proceed to examine witnesses and take testimony. If he be satisfied that there is sufficient cause for belief that the crime was committed and that the defendant committed it, he must hold him for the action of the grand jury. If he be not convinced he must discharge him from custody.

Even tho a defendant be discharged by a magistrate after examination, it is possible to go directly before the grand jury and re-present the case. An examination before a magistrate is not held with the aid of a jury and is preliminary in its nature.

Whenever a justice has discharged a defendant or has held him to answer for any indictable misdemeanor or felony, the justice must within five days return all papers in the case to the clerk of the county or supreme court having jurisdiction to try such case, and must also notify the district attorney of the county of all facts and a statement of the proceedings together with the names of all witnesses.

The Grand Jury

This is a body of men, not less than sixteen nor more than twenty-three, sworn to inquire into crimes committed or triable in the county. A grand jury is drawn for every term of the supreme court, and in cases of necessity may be drawn specially as conditions may demand. The grand jury sessions are secret and they hear evidence and testimony tending to establish the commission of crime, and decide whether or not a defendant shall be tried for an offense.

The papers in indictable misdemeanor and felony cases which were filed by the justice with the clerk of the court are presented to the district attorney when a grand jury is impaneled. The district attorney appears before the grand jury, producing witnesses who offer testimony as to the crime in question, and if the members of the grand jury be satisfied that there is probable cause to believe the defendant committed such crime, they return to the court a true bill or an indictment, charging the defendant with the crime and directing that he be tried for it before the county or the supreme court as the case may be. If they decide there is insufficient evidence they report no indictment and the prisoner must be discharged from custody. No evidence is receivable before a grand jury in defense of a person charged with crime.

Proceedings After Indictment

When a person has been indicted by a grand jury and a report of the indictment is returned to the county or supreme court, a bench warrant is issued by the judge of such court directing a peace officer to bring the defendant before the court. He is then arraigned on the indictment, the process of arraignment being similar to that in special sessions court, and he is required to plead to the offense. Should he plead guilty he is sentenced by the court, and should he plead not guilty he is given a trial. Trials in county or supreme court are held with a jury of twelve men and they agree unanimously on a verdict of either guilty or not guilty as the evidence may warrant. Should their verdict be guilty, the defendant is sentenced, and should it be not guilty, he must be immediately discharged from custody.

An appeal may be taken from a judgment of conviction in a county or supreme court to the Appellate Division of the Supreme Court, or to the Court of Appeals, and if such appeal is based upon a violation of constitutional rights it may be carried to the United States Supreme Court.

A peace officer should seek the advice and counsel of the district attorney especially in grand jury cases, for he is the officer charged with the prosecution and represents the people in criminal actions.

V

THE RULES OF CRIMINAL EVIDENCE

The rules of criminal evidence are mostly derived from judicial decisions laid down by the early courts of England and the United States, the greatest principle being the presumption of innocence; that is, that any person charged with crime, no matter how depraved and debased the person may be, is held innocent in the law until he is proven guilty.

The burden continually rests upon the prosecution throughout the trial to overcome this presumption and in order to overcome it the jury are strictly held by law to find the prisoner guilty of the crime charged beyond a reasonable doubt before he may be sentenced by the court.

If there is a reasonable doubt in the mind of any juror that the defendant is guilty of the crime as charged against him, it is the duty of that juror to hold out against a conviction provided his doubt is reasonably grounded on fact and such a doubt as a reasonable man would have upon the evidence presented.

The law further presumes that a man is sane until he is proven insane, living until he is proven dead, and in cases where the chastity of a woman is a factor she is assumed chaste until proved otherwise. It holds a child under the age of seven incapable of committing crime and presumes that a child between seven and twelve cannot understand the nature of a criminal act, which presumption must be removed by the prosecution.

It is common knowledge that persons who commit crime do all in their power to destroy evidences of the act, in order to prevent police authorities from arresting them, and to make proof of the act more difficult should they be prosecuted. Consequently, it has been necessary for the prosecution in very many criminal cases to resort to what is known as circumstantial evidence to prove the guilt of the accused. Crimes usually being committed in secret and without eye-witnesses present, circumstantial evidence becomes a most important branch of the law of the trial evidence in a case.

Circumstantial evidence alone is sufficient to support a verdict of guilty provided the jury believe that such evidence fastens the guilt upon the prisoner beyond a reasonable doubt. Nor is any greater degree of certainty required of circumstantial evidence than of direct evidence, for the same rule of reasonable doubt guides the jury in both kinds of evidence. There is no distinction made between the two kinds, and the jury are bound to weigh each kind. That is why a juror who has conscientious scruples against convicting on circumstantial evidence is readily excused by the court. Circumstantial evidence is sometimes stronger than direct evidence, for it has often been said that witnesses may lie, but that the circumstances in connection with the crime never can lie.

An example of direct evidence is the testimony of an eye-witness to a crime, while one of circumstantial evidence is the finding of a dead body, badly mutilated and the recovery of blood-stained personal property of the accused in the neighborhood, the appearance of guilt of the accused when discovered after the crime, etc.

Circumstantial evidence must be so convincing, however, that it must exclude every other supposition than that of guilt in order to be of value. Such as merely allows the jury to guess or speculate is of no value to the court in determining the guilt or innocence of an offender. In homicide cases it is sometimes difficult to prove the manner of the death of the deceased and it has been held in many states, including New York, that where the body of the victim was destroyed, it was not necessary to prove beyond a reasonable doubt the precise means by which the death was produced. The evidence of an accomplice in such a crime is always admissible to prove the crime itself and if corroborated, even by the confession of the accused, it may be sufficient to sustain a conviction. However, the uncorroborated evidence of an accomplice to a crime is insufficient to convict.

In every case of homicide, however, if a body is found or if any remains are found, they must be identified as those of the victim of the crime. The disappearance of the person supposed to have been killed with circumstantial evidence of the guilt of the accused will not sustain a conviction if the body is not identified.

A person accused of a crime is a competent witness in his own behalf and he may explain all the circumstances in connection with his action concerning the charge made against him. A person accused of crime, however, is not bound to take the stand or to testify, and his refusal so to do can not be interpreted as any indication of guilt.

One witness is sufficient to prove a crime against a defendant provided the jury are convinced that his testimony establishes the guilt of such defendant beyond a reasonable doubt. There are some exceptions to this, however, for in certain classes of crime corroboration of a prosecuting witness is required, as, for instance, in cases of seduction, rape, etc., no conviction may be had on the testimony of the female seduced or raped unsupported by other evidence.

It is not the number of witnesses produced at a trial which governs the verdict of a jury, but rather the weight of the testimony and evidence offered. A witness who testifies to a positive act, such as seeing a blow struck, is more liable to be believed than a witness who might give negative testimony—namely, that he was there at the time of the alleged assault but did not see a blow struck. It is, therefore, well to bear in mind that where you are gathering evidence you secure all the positive evidence possible, as this is the most valuable.

Altho it is better to produce in court primary evidence of the crime such as blood-stained clothing, the pistol or gun found at the scene of the alleged murder, still if these are destroyed or lost, evidence may still be produced by persons who had seen the blood-stains, the firearms, etc., upon the premises.

Any readily movable pieces of property which would serve as good evidence should be gathered up by police officers and *at once labeled or tagged for future use and identification.* Too much stress can not be laid on the proper marking of evidence and the memoranda which a police officer should make to enable him to testify intelligently at a later date. Such evidence is proper to be exhibited to the jury at the time of the trial as direct evidence of the fact, or to enable them better to understand the evidence and to make them realize its force more completely.

In the case of bulky objects, difficult of removal, the peace officer may describe such, but he can not give an accurate description unless he has properly prepared himself by referring to his notes just prior to taking the witness stand. Photographs of a scene of a crime are admissible as evidence, as are maps or drawings made by engineers. It is very advisable to obtain photographs, as a situation may change, and these are visible evidence of the original state of the case. Photographs are also admissible as primary evidence of the identity of persons alive or dead, to present the appearances of wounds, or to show that a child has been insufficiently fed or was ill treated and bruised. Photographs of bodies of drowned persons are likewise admissible to identify them in criminal cases. X-ray photographs are likewise of the greatest value in a trial to show the locations of bullets, etc. In case photographs can not be secured, a police officer may make diagrams and, if correct, they may be admitted in evidence.

In order to identify the defendant with a crime, any reasonable evidence which would convince an ordinary person of the connection of the defendant with the crime is admissible. Altho this is usually done by eye-witnesses or receivers of a confession, still even circumstantial evidence may be used to connect the defendant with the crime.

Wide range is given to such evidence. The witness may even go so far as to testify to the color, weight, or height of a person he saw in the neighborhood of where the crime was committed at the time in question, and the description may be compared with that of the accused by the jury.

The bad or quarrelsome character of the accused can not be shown by the prosecution unless the accused introduces evidence on his side to show his good character. By character is meant his general reputation from speech of the people in the community in which he lives, based upon his deportment and conduct. Except so far as the character of the accused for veracity may be attacked when he is a witness the prosecution can not show his bad character in the first instance unless he attempts to prove his good character. Evidence of good or bad character must be shown by the testimony of such persons only as have acquired the information from the acquaintance of the accused. The evidence must be as to the general reputation and not as to specific good or evil acts, and the evidence must show his character at or about the time of the alleged offense.

The prosecution must confine itself to proof upon the crime charged, as the defendant is not supposed to be prepared to meet other charges. An exception to this rule is when proof of the crime in question necessarily involves evidence as to another crime, as when the two criminal acts are mingled together.

The movements of the accused within a reasonable time prior to the instant of the crime in question are relevant to show that he was preparing for the crime; hence, it has been held on a trial for homicide that it is when necessary permissible to prove that the accused killed another person while preparing for the killing of the person for whose death he is being tried. Another exception is where the death was caused by some extraordinary or novel means and in such cases proof of similar prior crimes committed by the accused is admissible.

Declarations made by the accused at the time of the crime are admissible, as they show what was in the mind of the accused at the time. So also are the acts and declarations of the accused immediately preceding and following the crime. These are both admissible for and against the accused.

Altho hearsay evidence is inadmissible in both civil and criminal actions, certain exceptions to this rule exist. One of the most important in the criminal law is that of "dying declarations." Under this exception the victim of a homicide may make certain statements concerning the cause and circumstances of the crime, which statements are admissible coming from those to whom he made them, provided that the statements were uttered "under a fixed belief that his death was impending and is certain to follow within a short time and without opportunity for retraction and in the absence of all hopes of recovery." It is necessary to prove the mental and physical condition of the deceased as a preliminary to the proper admission of the evidence. The declaration must be of matters of fact and not of opinion, in fact must be only such facts as would be legally admissible if the deceased were living and testifying upon the stand. A statement that the killing was intentional or without reason or provocation or for no reason whatever are parts of the dying declaration which should not be allowed. The question of the admissibility of the dying declaration is a question for the court. The dying declaration may be even by signs.

Consciousness of Guilt: Any conduct of the accused near the time of the crime indicating a consciousness of guilt is admissible; his actions, general demeanor, language, mental and physical condition are admissible as circumstantial evidence of guilt. Similarly, lies told by the deceased, his avoiding giving information of his whereabout or about himself, his conduct when being arrested, his turning pale or attempting suicide are evidences of his guilt, also attempts to escape; his attempt to destroy evidence is likewise admissible; his silence when charged with the crime is also evidence of guilt.

Confessions: A confession is a voluntary statement made at any time by a person admitting the commission of or participation in a crime; it must be made without fear or promise and made freely and voluntarily; it must not be obtained by any sort of threat or violence, nor by any promise, and must not be influenced by hope or fear, and the court may hear evidence from both sides as to the conditions under which the confession was made. A confession in New York is assumed to be voluntary until the contrary is shown. The fact that the prisoner is confined does not make the confession involuntary. It is not necessary, however, to caution the prisoner in advance that the statement or confession may be used against him. A confession may be obtained by artifice provided the artifice and means employed were not calculated to cause the accused to make an untrue statement. The main point to be considered is "Was the confession probably true?"

Alibi: The plea is a plea of "not guilty" on the ground that the accused was at some other locality when the crime was committed. The burden of proving the alibi is upon the defendant and may be rebutted. The distance and period of absence from the locality in the alibi are very important when taken in connection with the time and place of the alleged crime. Celerity of travel also plays an important part. Alibis are regarded with suspicion by the court on the ground that they may be easily "framed up" and difficult of controversion.

Insanity and Intoxication: There is a presumption of law that a man is sane and responsible for his actions. This presumption is sufficient for prima facie proof by the prosecution and consequently makes the defendant prove insanity or intoxication so that he did not know the nature and quality of the act he was doing. When the accused presents evidence of insanity or intoxication sufficient to show that he did not know the nature of the act he was doing, the burden is then shifted back to the prosecution to prove the sanity and sobriety of the accused beyond a reasonable doubt. As to insanity, the evidence under the modern law has taken on a turn toward expert testimony in this regard altho testimony of non-experts is admissible to show the appearance and physical and mental capacity of the accused at the time of the alleged crime.

Privileged Communications: The names of persons giving information of crime to police officials need not be disclosed. It is now a matter of judicial discretion and will not be required unless absolutely necessary. Thus, also, are communications made to attorneys or their agents after the commission of a crime, but statements made to the attorney prior to the crime and preliminary thereto are not privileged. Information given to a physician by the patient, or by a person to a spiritual adviser, are also privileged provided they were acting in that capacity at the time. Confidential communications between husband and wife are also privileged.

VI

ASSAULT

An assault is a physical act of threatened violence against the person of another, which apparently might be accomplished, and if successfully accomplished, would effect a personal injury. The crime may be either a felony or a misdemeanor, depending on the manner in which the assault is made and the amount of force used. We will first consider the ways in which a felonious assault may be committed.

1. By assaulting a person with a loaded firearm, or any other deadly weapon, or by any other means or force likely to produce death.

Pointing a loaded gun at another and threatening to shoot is an assault within the meaning of this section, as is the aiming of a loaded pistol at a person, even tho, upon an attempt to shoot, it snaps and fails to go off. A deadly weapon is not one exclusively designed to take life or inflict bodily injury, for it is possible to use a baseball bat in such a manner as to render it a deadly weapon within the meaning of the statute.

2. By administering to or causing to be administered to by another any poison, drug, or medicine, destructive or noxious thing, chloroform, ether, laudanum or any other intoxicating, narcotic or anesthetic agent

when the use of such thing is dangerous to life or health, or when administered by a person to enable him or some other person to commit any crime.

3. By wilfully and wrongfully assaulting another in wounding or inflicting grievous bodily harm either with or without a weapon.

4. By assaulting another with intent to commit a felony against him or his property.

5. By assaulting a public officer in resisting or preventing the execution of any lawful process or mandate of any court or officer, or by assaulting such public officer to prevent the apprehension or detention of the person committing such assault or some other person.

It is important to note that whenever a weapon is used as a means of accomplishing an assault, irrespective of the degree of an injury, an arrest may be made for a felonious assault. The extent of the injury inflicted, in cases wherein no weapon or thing was used, will determine the grade of such assault. It is a question of judgment for the arresting officer to know whether serious or grievous bodily harm has been inflicted and whether the means used would be likely to cause such bodily harm.

The other class of assault referred to as simple assault is almost self-explanatory. It is a slight act of violence wherein no weapon or other thing is used and wherein the extent of harm caused the assaulted party is very slight and without any element of a serious injury. A blow struck at the face of an individual would be a simple assault, yet such blow if received in the eye or other vital part of the body wherein some temporary or permanent injury might be caused could be construed as a felonious assault.

Some assaults are not crimes and are justifiable in the following cases:

1. When *necessarily* committed by a public officer in the performance of a *legal* duty or by any other person assisting him or acting by his direction.

2. When necessarily committed by any person in arresting one who has committed a felony and delivering him into custody.

3. When committed by a party about to be injured or by another person in his aid or defense, in preventing or attempting to prevent an offense against his person, or a trespass or other unlawful interference with real or personal property in his lawful possession *if the force or violence used is not more than sufficient to prevent such offense.*

A person who is assaulted without provocation in a public place may, provided he does not kill his assailant, use sufficent force to repel the attack, altho he does not believe that he stands in danger of his life or grievous bodily injury and has an opportunity to run away. It is only when he kills his assailant that he is obliged to show that he stood in imminent danger of his life or of grievous bodily harm and that he could not avoid the encounter by running away.

4. When committed by a parent or the authorized agent of any parent, or by any guardian, master, or teacher, in the exercise of lawful authority to restrain or

correct his child, ward, apprentice, or scholar, and the force or violence used is reasonable in manner and moderate in degree.

5. When committed by a carrier of passengers, or the authorized agents or servants of such carrier, or by any person assisting them, at their request, in expelling from a carriage, railway-car, vessel or other vehicle, a passenger who refuses to obey a lawful and reasonable regulation prescribed for the conduct of passengers, if such vehicle has first been stopped and the force or violence used is not more than sufficient to expel the offending passenger with a reasonable regard to his personal safety. When a passenger on a train refuses to pay his fare, the conductor may use sufficient force to eject him, but the conductor must eject him in a manner consistent with his safety.

6. When committed by any person in preventing an idiot, lunatic, insane person or other person of unsound mind, including persons temporarily or partially deprived of reason, from committing an act dangerous to himself or to another, or in enforcing such restraint as is necessary for the protection of his person or for his restoration to health, during such period only as shall be necessary to obtain legal authority for the restraint or custody of his person.

A simple assault may also be committed by a person who operates or drives or directs or knowingly and wilfully permits any one subject to his commands to operate or drive any vehicle of any kind in a culpably negligent manner, whereby another suffers bodily injury.

VII

LARCENY

Larceny is the taking and carrying away unlawfully the property of another, or depriving or defrauding the true owner of the use or benefit of his property. It is essential in the crime of larceny that there be both a taking and a carrying away of property and that the intent be to steal.

Larceny may be either a felony or a misdemeanor, the former being designated as grand larceny and the latter as petit larceny. It is very essential that the policeman distinguish at a glance the degree of the larceny and the following simplified form will be of material assistance, if memorized. Each of the following is grand larceny and a stealing coming within any of these subdivisons is a felony:

1. The taking of any property irrespective of the value from the person of another. A pickpocket who was successful in extracting only one dollar from the pocket of a victim would commit grand larceny.

2. The taking of any property over the value of fifty dollars at any time and from any place.

3. The taking of any property over the value of twenty-five dollars in the *night time* from a vessel, railway-car, or dwelling house.

4. The taking of any public record or document.
5. Having been given goods to manufacture and appropriating such goods to the value of twenty-five dollars to one's own use without the consent of the owner.
6. Being an officer of a bank and accepting a deposit of more than twenty-five dollars, knowing the bank to be insolvent.

Every other larceny is a petit larceny, and consequently a misdemeanor.

Under a special provision of the penal law the stealing of any part of the realty or of any growing tree, plant, or produce is larceny and the degree will depend on the value of the article so stolen or severed. It is likewise larceny for a person to use a motor-vehicle without the consent of the owner and the degree of larceny is determined by the value of the vehicle so used. Larceny is also committed by obtaining money or goods upon a fraudulent order, draft or statement, or by false representation as to credit standing.

The operating of any coin-box or coin receptacle by the use of slugs or counterfeit coin and the receiving of service through such illegal procedure is an indictable misdemeanor.

A person who finds lost property under circumstances which give him knowledge or means of inquiry as to the true owner, and who appropriates such property to his use or to the use of another without having made every reasonable effort to find the owner and restore the property to him is guilty of larceny as of the value of the property. Bringing stolen property into the State is larceny, and even tho the stealing was accomplished in another State the prosecution may proceed here the same as if the larceny were committed within this State.

In ascertaining the value of stolen property the following should be observed:

1. If the thing stolen be an evidence of debt, the amount at stake because of its loss.

2. Railroad tickets and other such papers for passage on steamers, etc., the value of such ticket at selling price.

3. In every other case the market value of the article stolen irrespective of historic or intrinsic valuation.

The buying or receiving of stolen or wrongfully acquired property is a felony or a misdemeanor, depending upon the value of the property in question, provided that the person buying or receiving it, knows it to have been illegally acquired.

VIII

BURGLARY—UNLAWFUL ENTRY—BURGLARS' TOOLS

The word burglary is derived from "burgh" meaning a house and "laron" signifying a thief. Under the old common law a burglar was simply a house-thief, but our statutes have been extended and now the crime applies not only to houses but also to buildings, railway cars, vessels, booths, tents, shops, inclosed ginseng gardens, and to other erections and enclosures of the character used by mankind for the sheltering of himself or his property. In a broad sense a building within the meaning of the statutes on burglary has been held to include a structure having a roof and four sides. A dwelling house is a building, any part of which is usually occupied by a person for lodging therein at night.

The three elements necessary to constitute the crime of burglary are a break, an entry, and an intent to commit a crime, and unless they are all present there has been no burglary committed. We will examine first the element of break and the various ways in which a break may be completed.

First, we have a break by force wherein there is an actual breaking or detaching of any part of a building or of any covering thereof, or the opening of a window, door, shutter, or scuttle used to close an opening into such building. In other words, that is an actual breaking wherein some expenditure of the physical strength of the offender is necessary to make an opening. It is the most common sort of break, and generally it will be found on investigation of burglaries that the break was accomplished in this manner. There is, however, a constructive class of breaks wherein it is not necessary that the offender expend his human strength toward making the opening, and the first of these is breaking by aid or use of a threat or an artifice. We will assume that one desires to gain admittance to a house for the purpose of stealing some articles therein and to accomplish his object he rings the door-bell. The occupant of such house in response to the call appears at a glass panel in the front door, whereupon the thief pointing a revolver at such occupant demands that the door be opened and it is subsequently opened by the occupant. Altho the thief did not actually break the statutes, construe that by aid of the threat the door was opened for him and the element of break was therefore completed. In the use of a trick or an artifice one might falsely represent himself to be the agent of a telephone company, or a gas company, and through such misrepresentation be granted admission to premises by the occupants thereof. Altho the offender did not actually break into such premises by force, yet he gained admission through a false representation and this is held to be a break within the meaning of the statutes.

Employees or servants working within premises will

often plot with an outsider, whereby such servant or employee will leave a door standing open so that the outsider may walk into the building and commit a crime. This is a break by collusion, and both the person committing such burglary and the employee or servant are principals to the crime of burglary and through their collusion have completed the element of break.

A person who enters a building in any unusual manner for the purpose of committing a crime therein breaks when he does so. Going in through a pipe or a chimney or a coal-hole would in itself be sufficient, as the premises were entered in an unusual manner.

The element of entry is completed when the offender enters in whole, or when he inserts any part of his body or any instrument or weapon held in his hand into the premises, and a complete invasion of such premises is not necessary. In a recent case, a thief broke a window in a jewelry store and through the hole in the glass he inserted a fish-pole, extracting from the window several diamond rings on the end of the pole. Altho no part of his body was within the window it was held to be an entry, because the pole entered and such pole was held in his hand at the time.

The third element, "intent to commit a crime," is assumed. When one breaks into and enters premises unlawfully and has no legitimate purpose for being therein it is concluded that his intent is to commit a crime. Altho it is usual after a break and entry that a larceny is committed, yet it is not necessary that the thief steal property in order to commit burglary. He might commit any crime such as rape, homicide, malicious mischief, and for the additional crime committed he is liable for punishment in addition to the punishment for the burglary itself. It is also true that a burglar might break and enter an apartment house or an office building, and for this he has committed one burglary. After entering such premises should he break into several different apartments or offices he would commit an additional burglary each time he broke and entered. Each apartment or office is deemed a separate building for the purpose of the section.

Burglary is a felony and is always prosecuted by indictment.

Unlawful entry is the entering of a building or of any part thereof with intent to commit a felony, larceny, or malicious mischief, and is a misdemeanor. There is no punishment specified, so that upon conviction the maximum which might be imposed is a fine of five hundred dollars, or imprisonment in a county jail or penitentiary for one year. This is an indictable misdemeanor and can not be tried and determined in courts of special sessions unless jurisdiction is conferred especially on some city courts by charter. Unlike burglary the element of break is not necessary. In burglary the intent may be to commit any crime, while in unlawful entry the crime intended must be either a felony, larceny, or malicious mischief.

A person who makes or mends, or causes to be made or mended, or has in his possession in the day-time or night-time, any engine, machine, tool, false key, pick-lock, bit, nippers or implements adapted, designed, or commonly used for the commission of burglary, larceny, or other crime, under circumstances evincing an intent to use or employ, or allow the same to be used or employed, in the commission of a crime, or knowing that the same are intended to be so used, shall be guilty of a misdemeanor, and if he has previously been convicted of any crime, he is guilty of a felony. Under the above it has been held that where instruments are found on a person, adapted to the commission of the crime of burglary and the circumstances of the finding justify a belief that the intent was to use them to commit such a crime, the case is within this section even tho it were possible to use such instruments in a legitimate business.

IX

HOMICIDE

Homicide is the killing of one human being by the act, procurement, or omission of another and is divided into four classes, murder, manslaughter, excusable homicide, and justifiable homicide. No person may be convicted of murder or manslaughter unless the death of the person alleged to have been killed and the fact of the killing by the defendant, as alleged, are each established as independent facts; the former by direct proof and the latter beyond a reasonable doubt.

Murder in the first degree is punishable by death and may be committed in any one of the following ways:

From a deliberate and premeditated design to effect the death of the person killed, or of another;

By an act imminently dangerous to others, and evincing a depraved mind, regardless of human life, altho without a premeditated design to effect the death of any individual; or without a design to effect death, by a person engaged in the commission of, or in an attempt to commit a felony, either upon or affecting the person killed or otherwise;

When perpetrated in committing the crime of arson in the first degree:

A person who wilfully, by loosening, removing or displacing a rail, or by any other interference, wrecks, destroys, or so injures any car, tender, locomotive, or railway train or part thereof, while moving upon any railway in this State, whether operated by steam, electricity, or other motive power, as to thereby cause the death of a human being, is also guilty of murder in the first degree and punishable accordingly.

Such killing of a human being is murder in the second degree, when committed with a design to effect the death of the person killed, or of another, but without premeditation and deliberation. The minimum punishment for murder in the second degree is twenty years' imprisonment and the maximum is life.

Such homicide is manslaughter in the first degree, when committed without a design to effect death;

By a person engaged in committing, or attempting to commit, a misdemeanor, affecting the person or property, either of the person killed or of another.

In the heat of passion, but in a cruel and unusual manner, or by means of a dangerous weapon.

The wilful killing of an unborn quick child, by any injury committed upon the person of the mother of such child, is manslaughter in the first degree

A person who provides, supplies, or administers to a woman, whether pregnant or not, or who prescribes for, or advises or procures a woman to take any medicine, drug or substance, or who uses or employs, or causes to be used or employed, any instrument or other means, with intent thereby to procure the miscarriage of a woman, unless the same is necessary to preserve her life, in case the death of the woman, or any quick child of which she is pregnant, is thereby produced, is guilty of manslaughter in the first degree.

Manslaughter in the first degree is punishable by imprisonment for a term not exceeding twenty years.

Homicide is manslaughter in the second degree, when committed without a design to effect death:

1. By a person committing or attempting to commit a trespass, or other invasion of a private right, either of the person killed, or of another, not amounting to a crime; or,

2. In the heat of passion, but not by a dangerous weapon or by the use of means either cruel or unusual; or,

3. By any act, procurement or culpable negligence of any person, which, according to the provisions of this article, does not constitute the crime of murder in the first or second degree, nor manslaughter in the first degree.

Woman producing miscarriage. A woman quick with child, who takes or uses, or submits to the use of any drug, medicine, or substance, or any instrument or other means with intent to produce her own miscarriage, unless the same is necessary to preserve her own life, or that of the child whereof she is pregnant, if the death of such child is thereby produced is guilty of manslaughter in the second degree.

Negligent use of machinery. A person who, by any act of negligence or misconduct in a business or employment in which he is engaged, or in the use or management of any machinery, animals, or property of any kind, intrusted to his care, or under his control, or by any unlawful, negligent or reckless act, not specified by or coming within the foregoing provisions of this article, or the provisions of some other statute, occasions the death of a human being, is guilty of manslaughter in the second degree.

Mischievous animals. If the owner of a mischievous animal, knowing its propensities, wilfully suffers it to go at large, or keeps it without ordinary care, and the animal, while so at large, and not confined, kills a human being, who has taken all the precautions which the circumstances permitted to avoid the animal, the owner is guilty of manslaughter in the second degree.

Overloading passenger vessel. A person navigating a vessel for gain, who wilfully or negligently receives so many passengers or such a quantity of other lading on board the vessel, that, by means thereof, the vessel sinks, or is overset or injured, and thereby a human being is drowned, or otherwise killed, is guilty of manslaughter in the second degree.

Persons in charge of steamboats. A person having charge of a steamboat used for the conveyance of passengers, or of a boiler or engine thereof, who, from ignorance, recklessness, or gross neglect, or for the purpose of excelling any other boat in speed, creates, or allows to be created, such an undue quantity of steam as to burst the boiler, or other apparatus in which it is generated or contained, or to break any apparatus or machinery connected therewith, whereby the death of a human being is occasioned, is guilty of manslaughter in the second degree.

Persons in charge of steam-engines. An engineer or other person, having charge of a steam-boiler, steam-engine, or other apparatus for generating or applying steam, employed in a boat or railway, or in a manufactory, or in any mechanical works, who wilfully, or from ignorance or gross neglect, creates or allows to be created such an undue quantity of steam as to burst the boiler, engine or apparatus, or to cause any other accident, whereby the death of a human being is produced, is guilty of manslaughter in the second degree.

Acts of physicians while intoxicated. A physician or surgeon or person practicing as such, who, being in a state of intoxication, without a design to effect death, administers a poisonous drug or medicine, or does any other act as physician or surgeon, to another person, which produces the death of the latter, is guilty of manslaughter in the second degree.

Persons making or keeping gunpowder contrary to law. A person who makes or keeps gunpowder or any other explosive substance within a city or village, in any quantity or manner prohibited by law, or by ordinance of the city or village, if any explosion thereof occurs, whereby the death of a human being is occasioned, is guilty of manslaughter in the second degree.

Manslaughter in the second degree is punishable by

imprisonment for a term not exceeding fifteen years, or by a fine of not more than one thousand dollars, or by both.

Homicide is excusable when committed by accident and misfortune, in lawfully correcting a child or servant, or in doing any other lawful act, by lawful means, with ordinary caution, and without any unlawful intent.

Homicide is justifiable when committed by a public officer, or a person acting by his command and in his aid and assistance:

1. In obedience to the judgment of a competent court; or,

2. Necessarily, in overcoming actual resistance to the execution of the legal process, mandate or order of a court or officer, or in the discharge of a legal duty; or,

3. Necessarily, in retaking a prisoner who has committed, or has been arrested for, or convicted of a felony, and who has escaped or has been rescued, or in arresting a person who has committed a felony and is fleeing from justice; or in attempting by lawful ways and means to apprehend a person for a felony actually committed, or in lawfully suppressing a riot, or in lawfully preserving the peace.

Homicide is also justifiable when committed:

1. In the lawful defense of the slayer, or of his or her husband, wife, parent, child, brother, sister, master or servant, or of any other person in his presence or company, when there is reasonable ground to apprehend a design on the part of the person slain to commit a

felony, or to do some great personal injury to the slayer, or to any such person, and there is imminent danger of such design being accomplished ; or,

2. In the actual resistance of an attempt to commit a felony upon the slayer, in his presence, or upon or in a dwelling or other place of abode in which he is.

X

FELONIES

Abandonment   —Of a pregnant woman in destitute circumstances or liable to become a burden on the public.

—of children under the age of sixteen.

Abduction   —Unlawful taking or detention of any female for the purpose of marriage, concubinage or prostitution.

Abortion   —The miscarriage or premature delivery of a woman, who is quick with child, brought about with a malicious design or for an unlawful purpose.

-The selling or supplying of drugs or instruments to procure abortion.

—The killing of the child or the mother by means of the attempt to commit abortion is manslaughter.

Accessory   —To a felony is also guilty of a felony.

Accounts   —Falsification of, by public officers.

Anarchy   —Advocating the doctrine that organized government should be overthrown by force or violence, or by assassination of the executive head, or of any of the executive officials of government, or by any means.

Animals	—Administering or exposing poison so that it will be taken by any horse, mule or domestic cattle.
Arson	—Unlawfully and maliciously burning a building.
Assault	—When committed with a weapon or by means of a drug or by any means likely to produce serious or grievous bodily harm.
Automobiles	—Defacing identification marks.
	—using without lawful authority.
Bigamy	—The crime committed by a person who, having a lawful husband or wife living, marries another.
Blackmail	—The extortion of money or the procuring of an illegal act by a threat, in writing, toward criminal prosecution or the destruction of a person's reputation or social standing or personal injury.
Bribes	—Giving or offering to an executive officer.
	—executive officer asking or receiving bribe.
Burglary	—Breaking and entering a building with intent to commit a crime.
Evidence	—Forging or altering.
Extortion	—Obtaining property from another by a wrongful use of force or fear or under color of official right.

Forgery —The falsely making or materially altering, with intent to defraud, any writing, which, if genuine, might apparently be of legal efficacy or the foundation of a legal liability.

Homicide —The killing of a human being by the act, procurement or omission of another.

Kidnaping —The forceful abduction or stealing of a person.

Larceny —Where the value of the property stolen exceeds fifty dollars, or if stolen from a vessel, dwelling-house or railway-car in the night-time should the value exceed twenty-five dollars.

Maiming —Disfiguring a person or destroying or disabling any organ of his body.

Malicious mischief —Destroying or damaging any building or vessel by the use of explosives.

—wilfully burning any grain, grass or growing crop, standing timber, wild, waste or forest land.

—altering, extinguishing or removing any signal for the use of vessels or railway-trains.

—wilfully and maliciously destroying any property where the extent of such damage is more than two hundred and fifty dollars.

Rape   —Perpetrating an act of sexual intercourse with a female unsound of mind, or with a female against her will and by the use of force or with a female under the age of eighteen.

Riot   —An assemblage of three or more persons disturbing the peace by using force or violence to any other person or to property, or who threaten such acts and having the power of immediate execution of such threats.

Robbery   —The unlawful taking of personal property, from the person or in the presence of another, against his will, by means of force or violence or fear of injury, immediate or future.

XI

MISDEMEANORS

Accessory —There are no accessories in misdemeanors; all are principals.

Adultery —Sexual intercourse between two persons, either of whom is married to a
third person.

Advertisements —Concerning venereal diseases.

—to procure divorces.

—affixing to property without consent
of owner.

—untrue and misleading.

—concerning lotteries.

—placing advertisements on any object within the limits of any public
highway.

Animals —Abandonment of disabled.

—carrying in a cruel manner.

—keeping cows in unhealthy place and
feeding them unwholesome food.

—instigating fights between animals.

—overdriving, overloading, beating,
torturing, injuring, maiming, muti-
lating or killing cruelly.

—neglecting to furnish necessary food
and drink.

—administering or exposing poison to animal, other than horse, mule or domestic cattle.

—killing or trapping in burying-ground or public park.

Assault —When committed without a weapon and not inflicting serious or grievous bodily harm.

Assemblies —Unlawful when the intent is to commit any unlawful act by force, or to disturb the peace.

Automobiles —Assault if driven in a negligent manner whereby another suffers bodily injury.

—private use of seal or insignia of state or United States upon.

Barratry —Exciting groundless judicial proceedings in at least three instances.

Children —Endangering life, health or morals.

—permitting to attend prohibited resorts.

—omitting to provide for.

Civil rights —Discriminating against persons.

—refusing to receive guests and passengers.

—discriminating against United States uniform.

Disorderly conduct —Annoying or interfering with any person in any place by the use of disorderly language or by **any disor-**derly or offensive act.

Disorderly houses	—Keeping or maintaining.
Evidence	—Destroying.
Gambling	—Selling instruments or devices **for.**
	—keeping gaming and betting establishments.
	—keeping slot machines.
Hotel keepers	—Frauds on.
Larceny	—When the value of the property stolen is less than fifty dollars or if in the night-time from a vessel, dwelling-house or railway-car less than twenty-five dollars.
Malicious mischief	—Wilfully and maliciously destroying any property where the extent of the damage is less than two hundred and fifty dollars.
	—false alarms of fire or interfering with any fire alarm telegraph.
	—interfering with gas or electric meters or steam valves, water meters, water service pipes or their connections.
	—placing injurious substances in the highway.
Oppression	—By public officer.
Public officers	—Threatening to prevent performance of a duty.
	—impersonating peace officer.

—refusing to aid in making an arrest.

—resisting by the use of force or violence.

—exceeding authority in executing search warrant.

Public safety —Possessing or carrying any pistol or revolver without license therefor.

—discharging firearms in a public place.

XII

STATEMENTS AND CONFESSIONS

Very material assistance may be rendered prosecuting officers by the police in securing statements or confessions from persons accused of crime, especially in felony cases. A statement properly taken and in good form will be accepted as evidence, provided that it was made through the free will of the person accused and without the use of any force, duress, threat, or promise of leniency. Extreme caution is necessary that no right of the person be violated, bearing in mind that should it appear in any way that the prisoner's mind was influenced the statement can not be used in evidence.

Before taking a statement it is your duty to inform the person that such statement may be used against him in a criminal action, and if he choose not to speak he need not do so. Following is a ficticious statement, the general form of which may be used as a guide in preparing confessions:

STATE OF NEW YORK: ⎫
County of Rensselaer: ⎬ ss.:
Town of Brunswick: ⎭

John Doe, being duly sworn, deposes and says:

That he has been told by Peter Roe, the person taking this statement, that he need not make any statement unless he desires to do so; that everything he may say must be of his own free will and that anything he may say can be used against him in a criminal action. He does say as follows:

That he is thirty years of age, single, and resides at thirteen San Francisco St., Town of Brunswick, Rensselaer County, N. Y., and is a plumber employed by Sanford Hoe of the town, county and state aforesaid.

>That (here include what he may tell you of his part or connection with the crime in question, being very careful to get his statement exactly as he tells it).

>(After taking the statement of the crime use the following concluding paragraph for such statement.)

That the above statement has been made without any threat, fear, force, duress or promise of leniency and that it was so made in the presence of Peter Roe, Richard Goe and Thomas Moe.

That deponent has read the foregoing statement (or in case he can not read the English language, that the foregoing statement has been read to deponent by Peter Roe) (or in case he can not read or understand the English language, that the foregoing statement has been read to deponent in the Polish language by Stephen Igcewski) and that deponent swears that all and each and every part of it is true except such parts as are made on information and belief and those parts he verily believes are true. That he understands he is guilty of a crime should he swear to any false statement.

(Signature) JOHN DOE.

Subscribed and sworn to before me
this 15th day of April, 1922.
WILLIAM BOE,
Notary Public, Rensselaer County, N. Y.

>   The above statement made in presence of
>   (Signature) PETER ROE
>   (Signature) RICHARD GOE
>   (Signature) THOMAS MOE.

In the event that the deponent could not read the
English language and that the statement was read to
him by Peter Roe, include the following affidavit at the
bottom of the statement;

STATE OF NEW YORK: ⎫
County of Rensselaer: ⎬ss.:
Town of Brunswick: ⎭

Peter Roe, being duly sworn, deposes and says that
he resides in the Town of Brunswick, Rensselaer County,
N. Y., and that he read the foregoing statement to John
Doe, the deponent therein, said Doe being unable to read
the English language. That deponent did read such
statement to said Doe exactly as above written and that
said Doe did state to deponent that said statement was
true.

>   (Signature) PETER ROE.

Subscribed and sworn to before me
this 15th day of April, 1922.
WILLIAM BOE,
Notary Public, Rensselaer County, N. Y.

It is quite frequent that statements are secured through interpreters and in that case have the interpreter make the following affidavit at the close of the statement:

STATE OF NEW YORK: ⎫
County of Rensselaer: ⎬ss.:
Town of Brunswick: ⎭

Stephen Igcewski, being duly sworn, deposes and says that he resides in the Town of Brunswick, Rensselaer County, N. Y. That he read the foregoing statement to John Doe in the Polish language and that said Doe did state to deponent that said statement was true.

          (Signature) STEPHEN IGCEWSKI.

Subscribed and sworn to before me
this 15th day of April, 1922.
WILLIAM BOE,
Notary Public, Rensselaer County, N. Y.

It is advisable to have such a statement sworn to before some public officer authorized to administer oaths and also to have his seal impressed thereon should he possess one; however, if it be impossible to obtain the service of some such officer the statement made in the presence of witnesses will suffice.

Should it occur that the deponent be unable to write his name you may secure his mark provided that you have it witnessed. The following is the usual method:

        JOHN DOE (this may be signed by yourself).
        His (X) Mark

Witnessed by (signature) PETER ROE and (Signature) RICHARD GOE.

Ante-mortem statements, sometimes referred to as dying statements, are still another class which you will have to take. These are secured from an injured person and are for the purpose of incriminating the perpetrator of his injuries. A person making a dying statement *must firmly believe that he is about to die and can have no hope of recovery.* Unless this belief exists in his mind the ante-mortem statement can not be admitted as evidence and it is therefore recommended that in taking such a statement you ask the dying man the following questions, writing down his answers as he makes them to you:

> What is your name?
> Where do you live?
> Have you been injured and what was the cause of your injury?
> Do you believe that you are about to die as a result of your injuries and have you no hope of recovery?

You may then proceed to write such statement as he makes concerning the affair. This statement should always be made in the presence of one or more witnesses, and should the dying man accuse some particular person or persons with the act causing his injuries you should endeavor to have such persons so accused brought before him for identification before death. Of course this is not always possible, but such identification and accusation made in the presence of witnesses is very good evidence.

After taking the statement endeavor to have the dying man sign it, and his signature witnessed by at least one person other than yourself. It is also well to avoid the use of physicians or nurses as witnesses to ante-mortem statements.

XIII

SEARCH-WARRANTS

A search-warrant is an order signed by a magistrate, directed to a peace officer, commanding him to search for personal property and bring it before the magistrate. A search-warrant can not be issued except when there is probable cause for believing that the property is in a certain place, and the warrant must particularly describe the property to be seized and the place wherein search may be made.

In accepting a search-warrant a policeman must, therefore, examine it very carefully, taking great care not to seize any property not specified in the warrant, and only such parts of the premises as are specified in the warrant may be searched.

In securing a search-warrant it is necessary that the application be made under oath and it can not be issued unless there is probable cause. There are three instances wherein a search-warrant is permissible: First, it may be issued when the property described therein has been stolen or embezzled; second, when the property described therein was used as the means of committing a felony; third, when property is in the possession of any person who intends to use such property as a means of committing a public offense.

In serving a search-warrant, should you be refused admittance to the described premises, you may break open or into such premises, provided you have given due notice of your authority and your purpose, and have been unsuccessful in gaining entrance.

A search-warrant generally directs service in the day-time, but the magistrate may insert a provision whereby it is valid for day or night service. A search-warrant must be executed, except in the City and County of New York, within ten days after its issue, and after the expiration of such period the warrant is void.

There are special forms of search-warrants covering violations of the agricultural and liquor laws, but these are referred to in particular statutes which you may consult should you have occasion to secure one.

The officer in seizing property by virtue of a search-warrant must give a receipt to the person from whom the property was taken, or who is in charge of the premises from which it was seized; or, in case there be no person on said premises, he must leave a receipt in a conspicuous place thereon.

The property is then taken before a magistrate and the officer executes his return upon the warrant, such return being similar in character to the return made upon a warrant of arrest. The officer must likewise present to the court an inventory of the property so seized.

Too much care can not be exercised in the handling of search-warrants, and in each instance study your warrant carefully and only carry out the express directions therein contained, for it is plainly provided that a peace officer who exceeds his authority or exercises unnecessary severity in the execution of this process is guilty of a misdemeanor.

Search of premises may be made by an officer without a warrant provided the owner consents to have such search made; however, it is well to have some other witness present when such permission is given and likewise when such search is made.